DL
THE CLASSIC YEARS

Chine Publishing

Mark Chessell

Paddle Steamer 'Sandown' was a familiar sight on the busy Portsmouth to Ryde service from 1934 to 1966. She could carry 900 passengers. During WW2 'Sandown' was fitted out as a minesweeper and flak ship and evacuated many allied troops from Dunkirk in 1940. (Author's collection)

First published 2017
Published by: Chine Publishing
www.chinepublishing.co.uk

Printed by Shenzhen Jinhao Color Printing Co. Ltd
ISBN: 978-0-9573692-2-1
Copyright: Mark Chessell

Cover photo: 1960 Triumph Herald convertible VDL 632 (Nick Price)

Back cover: 1952 Austin A90 Atlantic saloon JDL 88 (Geoff Golding)

CONTENTS

INTRODUCTION AND ACKNOWLEDGEMENTS

Following the publication of "DL: Isle of Wight motor vehicles 1896 – 1939" numerous requests have been received from readers for a similar book covering the 1940s, 1950s and 1960s. This was a fascinating time for road transport development in the UK and is remembered fondly by many people. Car, bus, lorry and motorcycle sales were still dominated by British manufacturers. There were many makes, models, body styles and colours for customers to choose from, especially from the mid-1950s onwards.

On the Isle of Wight new vehicles registered by the Isle of Wight County Council continued to carry number plates incorporating the distinctive 'DL' county code. Virtually all of the restricted registrations during WW2 were in the DDL series. When numbers reached DDL 999 in March 1946 the council proceeded to issue EDL 1 – EDL 999, FDL 1 – FDL 999 and so on until YDL 999 was reached in November 1962. Then for fifteen months the Isle of Wight operated a 'reversed' numbering system (i.e. 1 ADL – 999 ADL, 1 BDL – 999 BDL and 1 CDL – 522 CDL). This was duly superseded by the year suffix letter system. From February 1964 new Isle of Wight registrations ran from ADL 1B onwards.

Almost 23,000 new motor vehicles were registered on the Isle of Wight between 3/9/1939 and February 1964. This compares with the estimated total of around 14,000 vehicles which were registered on the Island between December 1903 and 2/9/1939. "DL – The Classic Years" follows a similar format to "DL". There is a strong focus on clear images of DL-registered motor vehicles which were owned and used on the Island. Period photographs have been used wherever possible. These have been supplemented by some more recent pictures, virtually all of which are believed to be of vehicles carrying their original plates.

As with "DL" images of cars, buses, coaches, lorries, taxis, tractors, fire engines and motorcycles have been selected to illustrate the great variety of motor vehicles which carried DL number plates during this 25 year period. It has not been possible to include all the pictures I would have wished. I have endeavoured to provide a representative sample of vehicles which were an integral part of the Island scene in those days, including a few real rarities.

The photographs and historical information have come from many sources. The Isle of Wight Record Office, Carisbrooke Castle Museum, Isle of Wight Council, Isle of Wight County Press, Ventnor Heritage Centre, East Cowes Heritage Centre, W.J. Nigh and Sons Ltd. and Peter Relf have kindly permitted access to their marvellous photographic archives. I am also truly grateful to many people who have supplied some excellent images and information from their personal collections and have assisted on vehicle identification.

It is not possible to mention everybody by name but I would like to express particular gratitude to David Boon, Keith Brading, Jeremy Chessell, Sam Chessell, Marilyn Earley, Norman Fallick, Nigel Flux, Lucy Frontani of Carnegie Book Production, Geoff Golding, David Hales, Tim Harding, John Harrison, Felix Hetherington, Terry Jones, Geoff Morris, John Nash, Terry Nigh, Barry Price, Nick Price, Peter Relf, the late Bob Stay, Noel Stokoe, Colin Thomas, Don Vincent, Dave Warne, Martin Wallis and Chris Yendall. Most importantly I wish to give a huge thank you to my wife Susan who has been extremely supportive towards this research project during the past two years.

It is hoped that "DL – The Classic Years" will be appreciated by many local residents, visitors and classic motor vehicle enthusiasts. Every effort has been made to ensure that the information is accurate. If you do notice any errors or omissions it would be appreciated if you will report them to the author via the Chine Publishing email address (info@chinepublishing.co.uk).

Sutton, Surrey, October 2017   Mark Chessell

1 THE SECOND WORLD WAR (1939 – 1945)

From 1st January 1904 it became a legal requirement for all motor vehicles in the UK to carry a unique registration number. A system of two-letter area codes was introduced for all counties, cities and county boroughs and the Isle of Wight was allocated "DL". The Isle of Wight County Council was appointed as the local vehicle licensing authority and it was responsible for issuing numbers in the series DL 1 to DL 9999 in chronological order and for maintaining official records. Prior to 1921 a large number of the early registrations up to DL 2000 were reissued when vehicles left the Island or were scrapped.

The final two-letter DL registration number DL 9999 was issued on 10th October 1935 to a private owner in Yarmouth. Between this date and the beginning of the Second World War slightly over 3,000 new cars, motorcycles, buses, coaches, vans and lorries were delivered to the Isle of Wight and issued with three-letter registrations in the ADL, BDL and CDL series (i.e. ADL 1 – ADL 999, etc.). Virtually all of the CDL-registered vehicles took to the road in the period April 1938 to August 1939. Some of them were just a few months or even a few days old when the country found itself at war with Germany on 3rd September 1939.

During the final months of 1939 and the first few months of 1940 many private cars and motorcycles on the Island had to be laid up for the next six years. The following two photographs from the Carisbrooke Castle Museum archives illustrate a couple of such cars which were new in 1938 and 1939. Both vehicles were owned from new by Mr de Castel-Branco of Ryde, a keen and prolific amateur photographer.

CDL 146 *Standard 12 h.p. drop head coupe, supplied by Downing and Donovan Ltd. (Ryde Garage) to Mr Castel-Branco and first registered on 17th June 1938. (Carisbrooke Castle Museum)*

CDL 868 *Jaguar SS 2.5 or 3.5 litre drop head coupe, supplied by Downing and Donovan Ltd. (Ryde Garage) to Mr. Castel-Branco. This superb car was first registered on 23rd June 1939, ten weeks before the outbreak of WW2. (Carisbrooke Castle Museum)*

After the outbreak of the Second World War the British government introduced a range of national emergency regulations. These measures included the requirement for British research, development and production resources to concentrate on the 'war effort'. Most aviation, shipbuilding and motor manufacturing businesses were instructed to focus on the production of military aircraft, vessels and vehicles. Meanwhile armament factories were required to undergo rapid growth and improvements in productivity to provide the weapons and ammunition needed to fight a huge war in Europe and in many other parts of the world.

A small number of companies were given special permission to produce civilian vehicles during the war. These were restricted to 'essential' vehicles such as tractors, lorries, buses, fire engines, ambulances and police motorcycles. Three major bus manufacturers in this period were Guy, Daimler and Bedford. They were allowed to continue to produce chassis which were fitted with 'utility' bodywork (i.e. with basic angular designs and slatted wooden seats rather than upholstered seats). Park Royal and Duple were the main coachbuilders.

Being located in the English Channel to the south of Hampshire the Isle of Wight was in the front line of a possible invasion by Germany in 1940. In addition, the presence of major shipbuilding and aircraft manufacturing works at Cowes and East Cowes, the PLUTO pipeline at Shanklin (pipe line under the ocean) and the strategic radio communications facility at Ventnor meant that the Island would be targeted by many enemy bombing raids over the next few years. In order to provide protection for Portsmouth, Southampton and the Isle of Wight from possible attacks from the sea a number of coastal batteries and land forts were provided at the eastern and western tips of the Island. Three of the most important coastal batteries were at the Needles, Culver Down and Nodes Point, St Helens. All three were equipped with massive 9.2 inch guns and other heavy weaponry, and were ready for action when war was declared. Fortunately these guns never had to be used against the German navy. For an excellent detailed and illustrated account of the Isle of Wight during the Second World War please refer to Adrian Searle's book "Isle of Wight at War 1939 – 1945".

The photograph below shows a military training exercise at the Needles Battery in 1941. This major fortification was of paramount importance for guarding the western approach to the Solent. (Carisbrooke Castle Museum)

(Carisbrooke Castle Museum)

It was a very different story, however, with regard to bombing raids by the German air force (the Luftwaffe). Many anti-aircraft weapons were employed to defend Isle of Wight towns and the nearby ports of Portsmouth and Southampton from a number of major air raids. The largest and most concentrated air attack on the Island undoubtedly took place on the night of May 4th/5th 1942 when Cowes and East Cowes were subjected to a ferocious bombing raid. A total of 70 people in the two towns lost their lives and damage to industrial and residential properties was extensive. It would have been much worse, however, if the Cowes-built Polish destroyer Blyskawica had not provided such a resolute and effective defence of the towns. Throughout the whole war enemy bombing was reported in the Isle of Wight County Press in May 1945 as having resulted in 214 deaths, 274 serious injuries and the damage or destruction of almost 11,000 buildings, most of which were houses.

These two photographs show the 29th Independent Squadron, Reconnaissance Corps, 214 Infantry Brigade on training manoeuvres on the Isle of Wight prior to the D-Day landings in June 1944. In the upper picture a despatch rider on a BSA M20 500cc motorcycle is positioned behind a radio vehicle. The BSA M20 was produced from 1937 to 1955. It was the most numerous type produced for the British Army, Royal Navy and Royal Air Force in WW2 with 126,000 in active service. This reliable and easy to maintain motorcycle continued to be popular for civilian use into the mid-1950s, especially with sidecars. In the lower picture a sergeant crouches at the side of his armoured reconnaissance vehicle. (Carisbrooke Castle Museum)

On the Island the nationally important shipbuilding and aircraft manufacturing firms of J. Samuel White and Co. Ltd. and Saunders-Roe Ltd. were commissioned to produce ships and sea planes for the Royal Navy. Many male workers joined the Armed Forces and subsequently large numbers of local women, including the author's late mother Eileen Chessell (1921 – 1993), were trained as fitters to maintain a high level of production. Saunders-Roe Ltd. produced 480 Walrus and 290 Sea Otter sea planes during the war (see two Carisbrooke Castle Museum photos of Sea Otter production in East Cowes below).

The top national priority of pursuing the 'war effort' meant that several other strategic measures were introduced. These included a much greater self-sufficiency in food production (the land army), the requisitioning of land, buildings and transport resources to meet military needs and the rationing of food, petrol and clothing. Several new regulations resulted in major changes for road, rail and ferry transport and the use of public and private motor vehicles on the Isle of Wight. Beaches and seafront properties were declared out of bounds and private photography was virtually banned. Cross-Solent travel for civilians was highly restricted, especially in the final two years of the war, and people were unable to travel on the ferries unless they had a permit. These were normally only issued for travel in connection with war-related work.

Very early in the war petrol rationing was introduced and supplies were only available from a few authorised garages including Canning Day Ltd. of South Street, Newport. Scarce fuel was generally reserved for essential vehicles such as tractors, food delivery vans, buses, fire engines, ambulances, police motorcycles and lorries.

In the first few months of the war some civilian vehicles continued to make their way from factory production lines to garages around the country and local authorities were permitted to register them to businesses and individuals. On the Isle of Wight there were approximately 100 further registrations before wartime restrictions took full effect. Most of these new cars and commercial vehicles were supplied by Canning Day Ltd. and Frank Cheverton and Sons Ltd., both of Newport. They included DDL 15 (supplied by Canning Day Ltd. to Mr. A.C. Randall of Bonchurch on 6/9/39), DDL 21 (supplied by Canning Day Ltd. to Mr. Len Chessell of Northwood on 11/9/39) and DDL 20 (supplied by Frank Cheverton and Sons Ltd. to Mr. H. Fleming of Luccombe Farm on 12/9/39). In addition there were three late CDL registrations (CDL 950, supplied by Wight Motors Ltd. to Ryde Corporation on 5/10/39; CDL 990, supplied by Canning Day Ltd. to themselves on 1/10/39 and CDL 998, a Ford groundsman's tractor supplied by Frank Cheverton and Sons Ltd. to Mr. R.J. Flux of Shalfleet on 11/6/40 – see photo below).

(Keith Buckett collection)

11

Five new buses DDL 50 to DDL 54 were delivered to Southern Vectis on 1/1/1940. DDL 50 was a 56-seat Bristol K5G highbridge double deck vehicle while DDL 51 to DDL 54 were four 35-seat Bristol L5G single deck buses. DDL 50 operated as a conventional bus until 1959 when it was converted to an open top vehicle. In 1969 the vehicle underwent a second conversion by Southern Vectis into a tree lopper. After several years of additional service in this capacity DDL 50 was bought by bus preservationist Derek Priddle and beautifully restored to an open top bus.

DDL 50 *The upper picture (copyright Omnibus Society) shows this Southern Vectis Bristol K5G bus in its original livery outside the company's offices in St. James' Square, Newport. The lower picture (owner's collection) shows the same vehicle in service as an open top bus in Lake, probably in the mid-1960s.*

Original Isle of Wight County Council vehicle registration ledgers at the IW County Record Office reveal that approximately 750 new vehicles were registered on the Island during WW2. This information shows the date each vehicle was first registered, the name of the supplier and the name and town of the first owner. Unfortunately the make and model of vehicle were not recorded. Using the limited information available including photographic evidence, however, it is possible to make the following comments about the types of DDL-registered vehicles supplied from 1939 to 1945.

- Following the occupation of the Channel Islands in July 1940 the Isle of Wight boosted its production of potatoes and tomatoes and became an important supplier of these crops to the UK. There were well over 100 new DDL-registered tractors supplied to support the intensive production of food (e.g. DDL 386 to DDL 388 and DDL 394 to DDL 397 in October and November 1941). Many of these tractors were supplied to the Isle of Wight War Agriculture Executive Committee. Some other tractors were supplied direct to specific farms.

- Several fire engines were supplied to local fire brigades. Known DL-registered fire engines during this period were DDL 121 (Sandown and Shanklin Urban District Council), DDL 215 (Newport Fire Brigade), DDL 364 to DDL 366 (all Newport Fire Brigade) and DDL 369. It is almost certain that Cowes Urban District Council would also have had some new fire engines provided at this time.

- Seven Ariel 600cc motorcycles numbered DDL 272 to DDL 278 were delivered to the Isle of Wight police force on 21/9/40. These were supplied by C.F. Stagg of South Street, Newport to the Isle of Wight Standing Joint Committee and were allocated to different parts of the Island. The Newport motorcycle was kept just inside the front door of Borough Hall Garage in the High Street, in readiness for a quick response!

- Many lorries and vans were supplied to Isle of Wight businesses (haulage contactors, bakers, greengrocers, etc.) to enable them to continue serving local residents.

DDL 121 *was first registered by Sandown and Shanklin Urban District Council on 8th January 1940. (Carisbrooke Castle Museum)*

The railway network

At the end of the 1930s the Isle of Wight's network of steam railways operated by the Southern Railway had reached its maximum extent of 55 miles. From Newport there were lines radiating to Cowes, Ryde, Sandown, Ventnor West and Freshwater. In addition there was an important line down the east side of the Island from Ryde to Ventnor with a short branch from Brading to Bembridge. All lines continued to operate throughout the war and provided the main form of transport for essential trips between towns for local residents.

The rail services were particularly important for enabling thousands of people to travel to work in the major shipyards and aircraft works in Cowes. It was a real operational feat to manage the departure of four busy trains from Cowes to various parts of the Island around 5pm along the section of single track to Newport! The railways also played a key role in the later stages of the war carrying large numbers of allied soldiers who were garrisoned on the Island prior to the D-Day landings on 6th June 1944.

(Carisbrooke Castle Museum)

Local bus services

In September 1939 Southern Vectis (owned partly by the Southern Railway) was the largest bus operator. Shotters Ltd., Jack Wavell's Enterprise Bus Company and Seaview Services Ltd. were also significant operators. Shotters had two routes from Newport to Brighstone and Gunville, Enterprise ran from Newport to Sandown via Arreton and Seaview Services had a route from Ryde to Seaview. Other operators were Bartletts (Shanklin to Luccombe), Blake's Bus Service (Newport to Sandown via Newchurch), Cooper's and Pink Brothers in the West Wight and Meguyer and Nash who operated town services in Sandown and Ventnor.

Many buses and coaches were requisitioned in order to carry soldiers around the Island for training exercises and active service. This had a particularly major impact on Southern Vectis which lost the use of a large part of its fleet for the duration of the war.

All ten operators continued to run their local bus services to the best of their ability with their remaining vehicles, some of which were quite old. The wartime bus services provided a lifeline for many local residents, especially those living in the most rural areas. These services were supplemented by a number of carriers who transported goods and passengers between some villages and their nearest large town in their multi-purpose vans. Sightseeing tours of the Island by local coach operators were all suspended for the duration of the war.

According to recent research by local transport historians Don Vincent and Terry Jones fifteen new buses were delivered to the Isle of Wight between January 1940 and September 1945 (see Appendix 3 for details). Nine of these were allocated to Southern Vectis and six to other operators. The buses delivered between 1943 and 1945 were built to strict 'utility' specifications in order to economise on scarce raw materials.

DDL 649 *was a Bedford OWB bus with 32-seat Duple bodywork. It was first registered to Seaview Services Ltd. in April 1944 for its Ryde to Seaview route. (Alan B. Cross)*

DDL 759 was a Bristol K6A/ later K5G double deck bus with Duple utility bodywork. It was delivered new to Southern Vectis and first registered on 30/6/1945. It was photographed on 1st July 1946 at Ryde Esplanade on the route to Cowes. (Copyright Omnibus Society)

DDL 688 was a similar vehicle delivered new to Southern Vectis and first registered on 29/12/1944. It was rebodied by Eastern Coachworks with a lowbridge body in 1953. The bus went on to give a further 14 years of service on the Island until being withdrawn in 1967. It was photographed at Newport bus station in the mid-1960s. (Peter Relf)

Requisitioned vehicles

DL 7386 and DL 9700 *were two Southern Vectis buses which were requisitioned by the Ministry of Transport in April 1941. DL 7386 was an AEC Reliance with a 32-seat Dodson body, first registered on 18th March 1931. DL 9700 was one of a batch of thirteen 1935 Dennis Lancet 1's with Harrington 36-seat bodies. Four of these Lancets were requisitioned during WW2. (Carisbrooke Castle Museum)*

DL 8157 *was one of a pair of Bedford two ton lorries delivered new to greengrocer Fred Trim Ltd., Newport in November 1932. It was used during WW2 by the National Fire Service for towing trailer pumps. It is seen in this photo refilling with water at Ryde Canoe Lake. (Author's collection)*

E.H. Crinage lorry *(registration unknown).*
This large lorry is believed to have been owned by E.H. Crinage of Ventnor. Mr Crinage had extensive transport business activities on the Island and mainland, including a major contract to carry new engines from Coventry to the Morris factory at Cowley. The producer gas trailer suggests that the vehicle was being used on the Island during the war. (Ventnor Heritage Centre)

During the war and early post-war years the Women's Voluntary Service provided a range of valuable home care services to elderly people with limited mobility. This photo shows a WVS 'meals on wheels' delivery on the Island. (Carisbrooke Castle Museum)

ADL 506 *was a 1936 Southern Vectis Dennis Lancet with 36-seat bodywork by Eastern Counties. It is seen here with seven other buses and coaches collecting workers from the very large Saunders Roe Laminated Wood Products factory at Folly Works, Whippingham. This was an extremely important factory for the production of plywood and operated a three shift system during the war. (East Cowes Heritage Centre)*

CDL 109 *was a 1938 Burt's brewery lorry in Ventnor. In this wartime photograph it is seen transporting Home Guard soldiers. (Ventnor Heritage Centre)*

DDL 331 *is one of several wartime tractors to have survived at least seventy years. This 1941 Fordson is still in good working order and is shown taking part in a ploughing contest at Mottistone during the Easter weekend 2017. (Colin Thomas)*

DDL 607 *is another tractor survivor. This Fordson vehicle was bought new by Mr Thomas in 1943 for his Isle of Wight farm. It has the distinction that it has worked with the same family on the same farm continuously since that date and is now owned by Colin Thomas. In the above harvest time photo Colin's grandfather is on the left and his mother is at the wheel. At the back on the right are Colin's Uncle Don and his father, with Uncle Trev at the front. (Colin Thomas collection)*

DDL 215 *was a Leyland fire engine with detachable mobile long ladder. It was first registered on 17ᵗʰ May 1940 and was delivered to Newport Corporation for wartime service in and around the county town. (Author's collection)*

DDL 456 *is a large Thornycroft lorry which was delivered new in 1942 to C.B. Yates and Sons, haulage contactors of Merstone. This commercial vehicle has been restored and still exists. It was photographed at the Alton transport show in 2010. (Author)*

2 POST-WAR AUSTERITY (1946 – 1952)

The end of the Second World War in Europe was eagerly anticipated on the Isle of Wight in late 1944 and early 1945. It was duly greeted with much celebration on 7th May 1945. Many men who had served in the British armed forces would soon be permitted to return home and to rebuild the local economy and infrastructure. One of the first key challenges was to remove the extensive array of anti-invasion defences which had been installed along much of the Island's beaches and coastline. This was essential to ensure that the Isle of Wight could be 'open for business' again as a popular UK holiday destination.

According to P.C. Allen and A.B. MacLeod in their excellent book "Rails in the Isle of Wight" the Southern Railway operated a basic year-round timetable for the whole Island network between 1940 and 1944. This had been particularly heavily used by people from towns and villages who worked in the major shipyards and aircraft manufacturing works in Cowes. Fortunately the local lines, unlike those in many other parts of the UK, emerged from the war without substantial damage. They were not badly run down although they were clearly suffering from minimal wartime maintenance. On VE Day the total rolling stock consisted of 27 small steam locomotives, 121 coaches and 555 wagons of different sorts.

Immediately after the war the Southern Railway reintroduced a more frequent 'summer service' to cope with the expected influx of many thousands of holidaymakers. Allen and Macleod provide an illuminating description of how this operation was planned and implemented, based on the personal account of Gordon Nicholson who was the Southern Railway's Acting Manager for the Isle of Wight at the end of the war.

"The 1945 summer service was rather a triumph. I persuaded Waterloo that there would be a devil of a rush to the Island if the war was over in the spring and got carte blanche to run the best train service we could within the Island to marry with a basic hourly service from London (to Portsmouth Harbour). Of course the Island rolling stock was in fair order – unlike the mainland – and we put on what was almost a pre-war service, with three trains an hour on the Ventnor line. All this started on 7th May, which was also VE Day! In the result, both the ships and the trains carried an all-time record load that year. We started painting the engines green again before the end of the war and lining them out properly, wheels and all."

It took much longer for local road transport to recover to pre-war levels. Initially, the existing (predominantly pre-war) vehicles needed to be serviced and returned to active use, after having been laid up for nearly six years. These were augmented by large numbers of requisitioned buses, coaches and lorries which were returned by the military authorities to their former owners in various states of repair. Many of these were in poor condition. Coombes Brothers of Shanklin, for example, had two pre-war Dennis Lancet coaches (ADL 459 and ADL 573) returned after the war which needed extensive remedial attention before they were fit to carry holidaymakers on round-the-island tours and other excursions.

Bus and coach operators worked very hard to strengthen their fleets in order to meet increased passenger demand. This was especially important during the summer seasons from 1945 onwards when huge numbers of visitors from around the UK booked fortnight holidays at the Island's main seaside resorts and holiday camps. In order to cope with the high volumes of traffic operators made intensive use of their existing pre-war buses and coaches and purchased second hand vehicles from other quieter parts of the country. They also began to place orders for new buses and coaches but it took a couple of years before these began to come off the production lines in large numbers. The most popular and readily available coach in the 1940s was the 29-seat Bedford OB, normally supplied with Duple Vista bodywork. Between January 1946 and July 1950 almost eighty Bedford OB coaches were purchased by many local coach operators for round-the-Island tours, excursions to specific destinations such as Osborne House, Carisbrooke Castle and Alum Bay plus evening mystery tours. In order to obtain new vehicles more quickly in the late 1940s some firms arranged for locally built bus or coach bodies to be fitted to new lorry chassis (e.g. Morris Commercials and Dennis Paxes). This led to the introduction of some rare makes of public service vehicles alongside the ubiquitous Bristols and Bedfords.

The above photograph shows one of the numerous Bedford OB coaches supplied to Isle of Wight operators in the 1940s. FDL 318 was new to Seaview Services Ltd. in February 1948 and was pictured at Ryde Esplanade Coach Park. (Peter Relf)

There was a similar situation with regard to cars, motorcycles and commercial vehicles. Initially, new vehicles were in very short supply and there were long waiting lists for potential buyers. When people took delivery of new cars they had to sign a British Motor Traders' Association covenant that they would not resell them within three years. If these covenants were broken people could be barred from purchasing another new car for a certain period. Many early post-war vehicles were based on pre-war designs and some of these continued to be produced into the 1950s. Most Ford, Austin and Vauxhall cars followed this approach and their bodywork – with externally mounted headlamps and sidelights – began to look increasingly old fashioned. Other manufacturers, however, introduced streamlined models (e.g. the Standard Vanguard and Jowett Javelin) and set an example of sleeker design that other manufacturers would soon follow.

The flow of new vehicles gradually increased as the motor manufacturing companies restored large scale production of pre-war designs and introduced some new models. Under strict guidance from the Labour government manufacturers were encouraged to earmark a large proportion of new vehicles for the export market in order to earn the maximum amount of foreign currency. This national policy meant that shortages of new vehicles for the home market were extended into the early 1950s.

The situation was made even more difficult for British car buyers by the imposition of a 'super' rate of purchase tax on new cars costing over £999. Set at 66% this was double the standard rate of purchase tax for cars costing less than £999.

Immediately after the war the registration numbers DDL 750 to DDL 999 were issued up to March 1946. Many of these vehicles and some of the early EDL registrations were additional tractors supplied to the Isle of Wight War Agriculture Executive Committee. EDL 1 to EDL 999 were issued between March 1946 and July 1947. A large number of these vehicles were buses, coaches, commercial vehicles and taxis. Southern Vectis, for example, took delivery of twenty EDL-registered Bristol and Bedford buses and coaches to boost its ageing pre-war fleet.

New vehicles continued to be registered on the Island at a fairly slow rate up to the end of 1949 as the country edged out of the post-war austerity period. It is interesting to note that the average annual number of new vehicles registered from January 1946 to December 1949 was 660. This was over 100 fewer than the average annual number of new vehicles registered from January 1935 to December 1938 which was 770. From January 1950 to December 1952 the Isle of Wight saw a modest increase in new vehicle registrations and the average annual figure for this period rose to 930.

The photograph on the left was taken on Saturday 10th August 1963 and shows part of an enormous queue for the passenger ferry to Portsmouth. (Isle of Wight County Record Office)

GDL 765 *was a Leyland PD2 with Leyland 53-seat lowbridge body. It was delivered new to Seaview Services Ltd. in May 1950 and worked on the Ryde to Seaview route until it was withdrawn in November 1963. It was photographed at Ryde Esplanade some time before the wartime Southern Vectis Bristol K (DDL 688), bound for Alum Bay, received its replacement lowbridge body in 1953. (D.A. Jones)*

The period 1945 to 1952 was something of a 'golden age' for public transport providers across the Solent and on the Isle of Wight, especially during the summer months. The Isle of Wight was a very popular UK holiday destination prior to the advent of cheap overseas package holidays. Also car ownership levels were low. British Railways and Red Funnel ferries from Portsmouth to Ryde, Southampton to Cowes and Lymington to Yarmouth carried huge numbers of foot passengers at the beginning and end of their family holidays. Summer Saturdays were extremely busy and it was quite common for 30,000 people to travel each way through the biggest transport interchange point at Ryde Pier Head as the ferries provided frequent crossings to move the crowds. Most of the arriving visitors would swarm onto waiting trains to Sandown, Shanklin and Ventnor which departed around every twenty minutes.

Once they had arrived on the Island most holidaymakers made their way to their hotels, guest houses and holiday camps by train, bus or coach. By far the busiest railway line was from Ryde Pier Head to the major seaside resorts of Sandown, Shanklin and Ventnor. Local buses and taxis were ready to meet all trains and to take visitors on to their holiday accommodation. Two bus operators Meguyer (Sandown) and Nash (Ventnor) provided very useful flexible-route local services taking rail passengers to and from all parts of the towns.

As soon as the initial shortage of public service vehicles was overcome the various bus and coach operators provided an intensive array of passenger services for local residents and visitors. There were quite different levels of provision in summer and winter months with much more frequent services being run during the period May to September. For several years local bus services were provided by a number of different operators including Shotters Ltd., Jack Wavell's Enterprise Bus Service, Seaview Services Ltd., Blake's Bus Service, Bartlett's Garage Ltd. and the West Wight Motor Bus Company Ltd. Most of these firms, their vehicles and route licences were gradually taken over by the dominant operator Southern Vectis in the early 1950s. By June 1956 the only remaining independent bus operator on the Island was Seaview Services Ltd.. This firm continued to run its Ryde to Seaview service until 1992. For a detailed account of the Isle of Wight's independent bus operators please refer to "Independent Bus Services on the Isle of Wight" (Chine Publishing, 2012).

4411   The Esplanade, Ryde. I. W.

The above postcard photograph of Ryde Esplanade was probably taken immediately before the Second World War. It shows a busy street scene with several motor vehicles which would have been typical of that time and the period just after the war. The open top coach belonged to Newell's (Seaview) Ltd., which became Seaview Services Ltd. in 1942. (Copyright W.J. Nigh and Sons., Ltd., Shanklin, IW)

British Railways car ferry 'Lymington' was pictured at Yarmouth loading with motor vehicles and foot passengers prior to departure to Lymington in Hampshire. An FDL-registered Hillman Minx may be seen towards the fore of the vessel. The photograph is believed to have been taken in the late 1940s. (Copyright W.J. Nigh and Sons., Ltd., Shanklin, IW)

Round-the-Island coach tours

Prior to the Second World War many holidaymakers regarded a round-the-Island coach tour as an essential ingredient of their two week holiday. Such tours typically lasted for around seven hours and included stops for lunch and a cream tea. In the 1920s open top charabancs were used and these were generally replaced in the 1930s by coaches with sunshine rooves. When WW2 ended the Island coach operators (based mainly in Ryde, Sandown, Shanklin, Ventnor, Brighstone, Freshwater and Cowes) were quick to restart these lucrative regular excursions. Coaches all followed a clockwise route around the Island to minimise traffic hazards on the narrow country roads.

In addition to round-the-Island tours various additional full day and half day excursions and mystery tours were offered. The coach operators developed various methods of promoting these services and maximising ticket sales. These included ticket offices in the towns and on the seafronts plus agency arrangements with many hotels and local shops. Display boards showing tour destinations, departure and return times and prices were common.

The photograph below shows Nash's coach station in Pier Street, Ventnor. This well presented business premises in the centre of the town acted as an excellent shop window and sales point for the range of bus, coach and taxi services provided by the family business in the early 1950s. Round-the-Island tours cost nine shillings and six pence while half day tours to Carisbrooke Castle and Osborne House cost five shillings and nine pence. (Copyright W.J. Nigh and Sons Ltd., Shanklin, IW)

The above photograph shows a scene in Brighstone in the early 1950s with several round-the-Island coaches parked at a busy tea garden. The picture was taken from the top of Brighstone church tower. (Copyright W.J. Nigh and Sons Ltd., Shanklin, IW)

Isle of Wight Jowett cars and vans

Production of Jowett vehicles in Yorkshire resumed shortly after the Second World War. The two main models were the Jowett Javelin saloon and the Bradford van. Vehicles were supplied locally by Sandown Garage Company Ltd., Avenue Road, Sandown. Information about pre-war Jowetts on the Isle of Wight is extremely limited but one photograph in the author's collection shows a rare 1932 van which belonged to Sidney L Jolliffe who ran a household goods store in Atherley Road, Shanklin. Supplied by Davies' Garage, Shanklin it carried the registration number DL 8191 and was first registered on 1/12/1932. (see below)

The Bradford van had a fairly conventional design and was well known for its reliability and excellent performance, particularly in hilly areas. The following photograph, taken outside Sandown Garage around 1948, shows three FDL-registered Bradford vans which were quite popular with Island businesses. The Jowett Car Club estimates that around sixty such vehicles were sold on the Isle of Wight in the late 1940s and early 1950s.

(author's collection)

(Colin Thomas collection)

30

The Javelin, on the other hand, had a revolutionary streamlined design, and heralded the introduction of much more modern saloon car bodywork by other manufacturers in the post-war period. According to Jowett Car Club archive records 31 Javelin cars were supplied to Sandown Garage between September 1948 and June 1953. Comparing chassis number and first owner records with information in the Isle of Wight County Council vehicle registration ledgers it has been possible to identify the following 22 registration numbers which were issued to Javelins: FDL 838, FDL 926, GDL 412, GDL 673, GDL 938, HDL 51, HDL 105, HDL 234, HDL 312, HDL 324, HDL 325, HDL 449, HDL 546, HDL 547, HDL 678, HDL 796, HDL 830, HDL 843, HDL 911, HDL 912, JDL 16, JDL 59 and JDL 823. Interestingly eight Javelins were purchased on the Island by aircraft manufacturer Saunders Roe Ltd. of East Cowes and its subsidiary company SARO Laminated Wood Products Ltd. of Whippingham.

The Jowett Car Club has kindly supplied a picture of JDL 823. This car was painted black with brown leather trim. It was supplied by Sandown Garage to its first owner Dr. Sandiford of Newport. It was first registered on 2nd May 1953.

Jowett also produced a very stylish sports car in the early 1950s called the Jupiter. Less than 1,000 of these cars were produced up to the unfortunate demise of the company in 1955. One black Jupiter with beige leather interior, registered XME 740 in January 1952, is known to have been owned by a Mr Scovell in Ryde in the 1960s. According to Mr Scovell's daughter, her late father bought the car from Leslie's Motors in Ventnor as a 25th wedding anniversary present. She recalls driving the car on one occasion from Ryde to Totland Bay. The Jupiter was sold to Keith Brading around 1970. Keith Brading then sold and delivered the car to a man in Bradford, Yorkshire. The Jowett Car Club has confirmed that this classic car has been resprayed blue and still exists in fine condition (see photo below).

(Jowett Car Club archives)

(Noel Stokoe)

Taxis

Taxis provided another important component of the Isle of Wight transport system. Several bus and coach operators, commercial garages and taxi firms operated small fleets of taxis and limousines which were used to meet the varied needs of local residents and visitors. Typically large saloon cars were used as taxis (as opposed to purpose built taxis as in London). Business was particularly brisk in the summer months at the main ferry terminals, railway stations and hotels. In the immediate post war years some significant additional work was generated by passengers using the Ryde and Somerton (Cowes) Airports.

Although they were large in number relatively few photographs appear to have been taken of Isle of Wight taxis. Also the fact that most taxis in the 1940s and 1950s were standard saloon cars with very minor modifications made them hard to distinguish as the hackney carriage vehicles which they were. Several taxi operators from this period were Fountain Garage (Cowes), Wilf Barton (Newport), Henry Jolliffe (Gurnard), Coombes Brothers (Shanklin), Shotters Ltd. (Shanklin), Randall (Ventnor) and G.K. Nash (Ventnor). In his book on the fleet and company history of Shotters Ltd. Terry Jones records that Coombes Bothers operated a 7-seat long wheelbase Packard car with a 'straight eight' side valve 5.2 litre engine in 1935. This fine vehicle was used for private hire work for small groups before and after the war up to the sale of the company to Shotters Ltd. in 1949. Registered as BLH 243, the Packard was painted in Bronze and was immaculately maintained and turned out.

The following copyright photograph by W.J. Nigh and Sons Ltd. shows three of G.K. Nash's taxis, all pre-war Austins, taken at the junction of Steephill Road and Castle Road, very close to the entrance to the former Ventnor West station. This was the terminus of the line from Newport via Merstone Junction, Godshill, Whitwell and St Lawrence which closed in September 1952. From left to right the taxis are DCD 531 (a Brighton-registered Austin 4-cylinder 12 or 14 saloon), ADL 17 (an Austin 18 York saloon) and CAD 82 (a Gloucestershire-registered Austin 16 or 18 Chalfont limousine). It is believed to have been taken in the spring of 1952 a few months before the branch line closed. ADL 17 was first registered on 23rd October 1935. It was supplied by Frank Cheverton Ltd. to Mrs M.G. Thornton, Penshurst, Blackwater. The original garage billhead reveals that this attractive vehicle was black and brown when new, its chassis number was 40995/18 and its car number was E/RP.2799/18.

John Nash's Ventnor transport memories

John Nash, the son of G.K. (Gerry) Nash, was born in June 1921. His father had built up a large and diverse transport business in Ventnor before the war. This included a local bus service (Brown's Bus), coach excursions, the sale of new and second hand cars (especially Morris and Citroen), a taxi service, motor repairs and a vehicle recovery facility. During the war the coach excursions and car sales were put into mothballs but the firm continued to operate its local bus service and taxis in and around the town. In addition Gerry Nash was appointed as the Transport Officer for Ventnor and he was responsible for coordinating transport services in the area to meet special wartime requirements.

John had a five year engineering apprenticeship at the Royal Aircraft Establishment in Farnborough from 1937 to 1942. He worked long hours during the war and was unable to travel back to visit his family very often, but he did manage to return to Ventnor several times. Portsmouth and Southampton were bombed heavily for several years and John had to try to identify lulls in the attacks for his trips across the Solent. On one rare weekend off in August 1942 John was in Ventnor and was walking down Pier Street to go to the Winter Gardens. This large building was being used as a canteen for soldiers based in the area. He saw three aircraft heading towards the town from over the English Channel. Initially he thought they were RAF Typhoons but he then realised they were German Fokke Wolf 190s. He was just able to dive behind a wall before the planes fired bullets into the town centre and dropped a 500lb bomb which caused considerable damage and some serious injuries.

After the war Ventnor soon regained its status as a bustling seaside town with many local attractions and an excellent sunshine record. Most of the holidaymakers arrived by train from Ryde and Nash's town bus service and taxis were kept very busy during the summer months carrying families to and from their hotels and guest houses. The coach excursions resumed quickly, using pre-war vehicles which had been kept in storage, and these were replaced by six new coaches over the next five years – two Dennis Lancet J3s with Duple bodywork (EDL 715 and FDL 216), a Bedford OB with Duple Vista bodywork (FDL 713), two Crossley SD42-7s with Whitson bodywork (GDL 32 and GDL 33) and a Commer Avenger 23A with Harrington bodywork (HDL 304). The pre-war livery of bright red was changed to cream and pale green. Nash's garage business became active again for the sale of new and used cars and the servicing and repair of vehicles.

In 1949 Gerry Nash experienced a serious case of peritonitis and was unable to work for several months. Although he was employed in a senior position on the mainland John offered to give up his job and return to the Island to manage the family business. Originally he thought that this arrangement would last for a year or so but as events turned out he worked alongside his father for six years. Coach excursions formed a major part of the business in the early 1950s and there was fierce competition with two other established coach operators in Ventnor – Randalls and Crinages. John remembers introducing several new methods for winning additional customers. One of the most successful approaches was to offer local hotels a 10% commission for each Nash ticket sold. Another innovation was the design of a special promotional console. This contained a large map of the Isle of Wight which was illuminated by a series of small light bulbs showing the coach excursion routes and it was positioned strategically at the entrance to the coach station. A third marketing initiative was introduced to coincide with the departure of the firm's fleet of coaches at 10am each day to various destinations around the Island. Just as the coaches set off the loudspeaker system broadcast the famous tune "The Post Horn Gallop". This dramatic spectacle created much excitement for the departing passengers and generated a lot of additional ticket sales to other holidaymakers for future excursions!

Around 1955 Gerry Nash took the decision to sell the Ventnor town bus service and coach excursions business to Southern Vectis and this major change took place in June 1956. The sale included the centrally located Pier Street coach station and five post-war coaches, all of which were in excellent condition. Southern Vectis continued to use these former Nash vehicles for their coach excursions until 1960. From 1956 until the company closed in 1970 Gerry Nash concentrated on the garage, petrol sales and taxi service aspects of the business.

The final coach to be purchased by G.K. Nash (in May 1951) was HDL 304, a 33-seat Commer Avenger with attractive Harrington bodywork. It was pictured at the Grove Road car park in Ventnor. (Copyright W.J. Nigh and Sons Ltd., Shanklin, IW)

EDL 325 *was a yellow Aveling Barford road roller. It was first registered on 30/8/1946 and was supplied to Ryde Corporation by the manufacturer. This photograph was taken on 23/11/1974 at Ryde Esplanade when the vehicle was still in active service repairing local roads almost thirty years after it was built. (Peter Relf)*

DL 8313 *was a Ford AA 14-seat bus. It was first registered on 25/3/1933 to H.J. Saunders of Ventnor. The vehicle was later sold to R.H. Chapman of Cowes who used it as a van. After the war the vehicle passed to Harry Blake of Newport who operated a carrier bus service from Newport to Sandown via Newchurch. It is believed that Mr. Blake mainly used the vehicle as a van between 1947 and 1952, when there were still many pre-war vehicles in use on the Island. (Author's collection)*

EDL 640 *was a Bedford OB bus with a Duple B26F body. It was built in 1947 and was delivered new to Southern Vectis. In this photograph it is working on the Newport town service 15A. The vehicle is turning right from Pyle Street into St James' Square. In 2017 this section of Pyle Street is now one-way in the other direction. (Author's collection)*

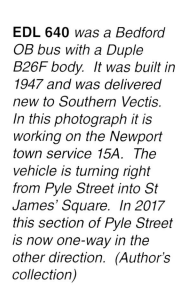

EDL 774 *was an early post-war Singer 9 h.p. roadster. It was first registered on 8/4/1947 when there were very few new cars available on the Island. The first owner was Chester Lawrence of Ryde and the car was supplied by Westridge Service Station.*
(Carisbrooke Castle Museum)

EDL 946 *is a Vauxhall J14 saloon. This car was first registered on 1/7/1947 to a Mr Bassett of Ryde and was supplied by Westridge Service Station. It had a 1781cc six cylinder engine and three speed gearbox. This car still exists on the Island and is in excellent roadworthy condition. It has had several owners and has been restored at least twice. The current owner is Colin Thomas and he purchased the car from Eddie James in 2001. Note the fluted bonnet which was a distinctive feature of Vauxhall cars for many years. (Colin Thomas)*

FDL 64 *was one of a pair of new Daimler CVD6 buses with a 35-seat Willowbrook body. The two buses (FDL 63 and FDL 64) were ordered direct by Shotters Ltd. in July 1947 and were delivered in October 1947. Shotters Ltd. purchased 11 new FDL-registered buses and coaches in 1947 and 1948 (FDL 63 – FDL 70, FDL 432, FDL 433 and FDL 577). Alongside the two Daimler buses these fleet acquisitions comprised three Daimler CVD6 coaches with 32-seat bodies, four Bedford OB coaches with 26-seat Pearson or 29-seat Duple bodies and two Dennis Lancet J3 coaches with 35-seat bodies. FDL 63 and FDL 64 worked on Shotters' two local bus services from Newport to Gunville and Brighstone/Compton Bay from 1947 until the two route licences were sold to Southern Vectis in May 1956. The photograph was taken in St. James' Square, Newport in 1951. (Alan B. Cross)*

FDL 451 *is a Hillman Minx convertible. It was first registered on 6/5/1948. The car was supplied by Wight Motors Ltd. to a Mr. Tulloch of Ryde. It is believed that the vehicle still exists on the Island with its original DL registration number. (Colin Thomas collection)*

FDL 896 *was a Ford general purpose lorry owned by Cowes Urban District Council. It was supplied to the Council by Holmes' Garage in Cowes and was first registered on 17/1/1949. The photograph was taken in Cowes High Street when flooding was quite a common event. (Isle of Wight County Record Office)*

GDL 107 was a Triumph Renown saloon, probably a 2000 TDA model. Its first owner was Mr de Castel-Branco of Ryde. He bought the car from Downing and Donovan Ltd. (Ryde Garage) and it was first registered on 2/5/1949. Mr de Castel-Branco took many photographs of this car in different parts of the Island. They form part of his huge collection of images from the 1930s to the 1950s which was donated to the Carisbrooke Castle Museum. The front and rear view photographs on this page are believed to have been taken on the Military Road.

The upper view of GDL 107 on this page may have been taken outside the owner's home in St Thomas Street, Ryde. The lower view shows the Triumph Renown waiting at Alverstone level crossing for a train being hauled by British Railways class 02 type 0-4-4 locomotive 'Bembridge', built in 1892, to pass by. Alverstone station was on the branch line from Newport to Sandown which closed in February 1956. (Carisbrooke Castle Museum)

GDL 402 *is a Bedford OL lorry which was a popular commercial vehicle in the late 1940s and early 1950s. Supplied by Canning Day Ltd. it was first registered on 1/11/1949. The first owners of the lorry were David Day and Sons in Bonchurch. This vehicle still exists on the Isle of Wight and is now owned by Tim Day. The vehicle may often be seen at the Isle of Wight Military Museum at Northwood and at several transport shows during the summer months. (Author)*

GDL 435 *was a Bristol K5G bus with Eastern Coachworks 55-seat lowbridge body, new to Southern Vectis in 1950. This vehicle was one of a pair of Bristol double deck buses (together with GDL 434) diverted to the Isle of Wight from Caledonian Omnibus Company Ltd., Dumfries. This photograph was taken in July 1964 at Steephill Road, Ventnor. (Peter Relf)*

GCR 447 *is a Seddon lorry which was new in 1949 and still exists in excellent condition. Although it was issued with a Southampton registration it is considered as an Isle of Wight vehicle and has spent virtually all of its life on the Island. It was supplied to Mew, Langton and Co. Ltd., Royal Brewery, Crocker Street, Newport where it joined two other Seddon lorries from the early 1940s (both of which still exist). Seddon produced a range of durable buses and commercial vehicles in the 1940s and 1950s but did not have a dealer or agent on the Isle of Wight. Mew Langtons therefore purchased the lorry through the nearest distributor, Messrs Tilbury, Western Esplanade, Southampton. The vehicle was supplied as a flatbed lorry and was modified on arrival by brewery maintenance staff to make it more suitable for carrying kegs of beer, cases of wine and other bulky items to public houses around the Island. The lorry had a long and active working life with Mew Langtons and was sold in 1968 to a farmer in Yafford who used it mainly for work on his farm for a further 15 years. The vehicle was then sold to a man in Wroxall who kept it under cover until 2006, when it was sold to its present owner Bill Steward. Mr Steward then carried out a complete restoration of the vehicle in three years, between 2009 and 2012. This rare and attractive commercial vehicle now attends around six shows each year. It is very popular with local residents and visitors, partly as a result of the important role it played as a working vehicle on the Island for almost 35 years. The only known Seddon vehicle with a DL registration was the Seddon Mk 4 bus with a Whitson FB31F body. This bus (GDL 158) was supplied direct to Shotters Ltd. in July 1949 and it had the distinction of operating the final journey on the firm's route from Newport to Brighstone and Brook in May 1956. (Bill Steward)*

GDL 462 *is a Nuffield tractor, supplied by Fowler's Ltd.. It was first registered on 1/11/1949 and its fist owner was Mr Buckingham of Newport. This tractor still exists on the Isle of Wight. (Colin Thomas)*

GDL 599 *was a Ford van supplied by Frank Cheverton Ltd. to themselves. The vehicle was first registered on 27/3/1950 and was one of several vehicles employed by the company for the mobile servicing of Fordson tractors on customers' farms. This photograph was taken in the Carisbrooke Castle car park. (Barry Price collection)*

GDL 705 *was a Jaguar Mk 5 saloon and was surely one of the most stylish cars to be seen on the Isle of Wight in the early 1950s. The prestigious vehicle was supplied by Bartletts' Garage. It was first registered on 27/3/1950 and its first owner was a Mr Browning of Totland. Unfortunately little is known about the history of this car but it is believed that it still exists, possibly in the Channel Islands. (Author's collection)*

GDL 722 *was a coal delivery lorry for Wood and Jolliffe Ltd. in Newport in the 1950s. It was first registered on 13/4/1950 and was supplied by Gubbins and Ball Ltd., Newport to themselves. In this photograph at Newport railway station the lorry is seen alongside a horse drawn wagon which was also used by Wood and Jolliffe Ltd. for coal deliveries in Newport at that time. (Isle of Wight County Record Office)*

GDL 764 *was one of a pair of Leyland PD2s with a 53-seat Leyland lowbridge body supplied new to Seaview Services Ltd. in May 1950. Together with its sister bus (GDL 765) this vehicle worked regularly on the firm's busy route from Ryde to Seaview via Puckpool Park. GDL 765 was withdrawn in 1963 and was replaced by an unusual Bedford VAL with 54-seat Willowbrook bus bodywork (ADL 321B). GDL 764 continued in service until 1971 and was photographed at Ryde Esplanade in front of 1954 Southern Vectis Bristol Lodekka JDL 996. It has since been restored by Derek Hunt and may often be seen at the Isle of Wight Bus and Coach Museum in Ryde. (Upper picture Peter Relf, lower picture author)*

DL 9065 *was another pre-war bus which continued to see active operational service on the Isle of Wight in the 1950s. It was a Dennis Ace with Duple 20-seat body and was delivered new to Shotters Ltd. in June 1934. The bus was sold to Meguyer in Sandown in 1948 and then resold to G.K. Nash in Ventnor in June 1950. For a further five years this sturdy vehicle worked intensively on the Ventnor town service (Brown's Bus) with regular driver Bill Turner normally at the wheel. (Copyright Omnibus Society)*

HDL 278 *is a Lanchester Ten LD10 with Barker sports saloon body. This car had a 1287c.c. engine and was first registered on 6/2/1951. It was supplied by Fowler's Ltd. and its first owner was a Mr Stainer of Ryde. Lanchester produced the first British motor car in 1895/96. The company was taken over by BSA in 1930 and various Lanchester models continued to be built in the West Midlands up to 1955. HDL 278 still exists on the mainland. These photographs were taken at the Alton Transport Show in 2010. (Author)*

HDL 279 *is a Bristol LL5G rear entrance single deck bus with Eastern Coachworks 39-seat body. It was first registered on 1/6/1952 and was one of 12 such vehicles supplied to Southern Vectis between 1950 and 1952. The final batch of these 30 foot vehicles are believed to have been the last rear entrance single deck buses to be manufactured by Bristol. All 12 of these buses were sold between 1963 and 1966, partly because they were unsuitable for conversion to one person operation. Three of these buses, including HDL 279, still exist. HDL 279 was sold to Jeffries, a Southampton dealer, in 1966 who sold the bus to construction company Reema in Salisbury. Around 1973 the bus was purchased by an Isle of Wight bus enthusiast. In the late 1990s he sold the vehicle to a member of the Isle of Wight Bus and Coach Museum who repainted it. Sadly this man died in 2000 and his family sold HDL 279 to Bill Steward, an experienced vehicle preservationist on the Island. Over the next six years Bill Steward carried out a full and meticulous restoration of this rare bus in his workshop. A lot of mechanical work was carried out and the body was almost completely rebuilt and refurbished, including the reupholstering of all 39 seats with authentic moquette material. The vintage bus is now in excellent condition and attends a number of transport events at the Isle of Wight Bus and Coach Museum and Isle of Wight Steam Railway at Havenstreet each year. (Bill Steward)*

These three photographs show HDL 279 before and during its restoration. This was a major project which required great skill, determination and attention to detail over a six year period. (Bill Steward)

HDL 699 *is a Bedford general purpose open lorry which was first registered on 13/8/1951. This commercial vehicle was supplied by Canning Day Ltd. to the Isle of Wight County Council Highways Department. The lorry still exists and is currently owned by Tim Day on the Island. (Colin Thomas collection)*

JDL 40 *was a Bristol K double deck bus delivered to Southern Vectis in the summer of 1952. It was one of 15 Bristol KSW5G vehicles bought new in 1952/53 (JDL 33 – 42, and JDL 719 – 723) and was supplied with a 55-seat lowbridge body by Eastern Coachworks. These were the final new Bristol K buses bought by the company before they invested in a large number of Bristol Lodekka buses over the next 15 years. JDL 40 provided almost 20 years of service on the Island before being sold around 1970. (Author's collection)*

JDL 48 *was one of a batch of five Bristol LS6G coaches with 39-seat Eastern Coachworks bodies purchased by Southern Vectis in 1952 (JDL 44 – 48). It was photographed in the centre of Godshill on a well-patronised sightseeing excursion to Alum Bay and the Needles. (Alan B. Cross)*

JDL 48 *and its four sister coaches were rebodied and converted into 37-seat vehicles in 1966. They then became suitable for use as one-person-operated buses and were mainly employed on local bus services until they were sold in 1970/71. (Copyright Brian Botley)*

JDL 88 *was a rare Austin A90 Atlantic fabric-covered hard top sports saloon. These futuristic cars (some of which were produced in convertible form) were built by Austin from 1949 to 1952. Around 8,000 were made in total, with almost 3,600 of these for export. The cars had a 2660c.c. engine and incorporated a number of novel features, including three headlights, hydraulically powered windows, flashing indicators and an opening central rear window. JDL 88 was first registered on 7/4/1952.*

It was supplied by Frank Cheverton Ltd. and its first owner was a Mr Ball of Newport. This fine vehicle was restored and repainted on the Isle of Wight in the 1990s. Geoff Golding carried out some major mechanical repairs on the car for its Bembridge owner in 1996, and took these two photographs prior to it being sold. This vehicle may still exist but its current whereabouts are unknown. (Geoff Golding)

JDL 104 *was a Vauxhall Wyvern with a distinctive fluted Vauxhall bonnet. This car was first registered on 10/4/1952. It was supplied by Canning Day Ltd. to Mr John Snellgrove, a Newport businessman and keen rally driver. Mr Snellgrove drove the car in the April 1953 Isle of Wight Car Rally. The first photograph shows a reverse hill climbing test in Sandown. The second picture shows JDL 104 as it looked during the concours d'elegance stage of the rally. The final photograph shows John Snellgrove with several rally trophies outside Canning Day Ltd.'s Vauxhall garage in Church Litten, Newport. (Philip Snellgrove collection)*

JDL 506 *was an Austin A40 Somerset saloon. This car was probably first registered in late 1952 and is possibly a limited edition, higher performance sports model as indicated by the two tone paintwork. Its supplier and first owner are unknown because the page containing information on this vehicle is missing from the original IWCC vehicle registration ledger in the County Record Office. When this photograph was taken in May 1974 the car's bodywork still appeared to be in good condition apart from the absence of a rear hubcap. (Peter Relf)*

3 ECONOMIC PROSPERITY (1953 – 1964)

After seven long years of austerity the domestic market for private motor vehicles began to show clear signs of recovery. Many firms and individuals were ready and able to invest in a new car, motorcycle or van, often for the first time. British motor manufacturers, especially the largest companies Morris, Austin, Ford, Vauxhall and the Rootes Group (including Hillman, Humber, Sunbeam and Singer) were quick to respond to the major increase in demand and expanded their production capacity accordingly.

Other motor manufacturers including Rover, Standard, Triumph and Wolseley also sought to boost their vehicle production but found it increasingly difficult to compete with the mass production and marketing of their larger competitors. Jowett, for example, was forced to cease production in the mid-1950s, partly because the firm lost its access to the major bodymaking factory of Briggs of Doncaster to a rapidly growing Ford Motor Company. In addition there was some limited competition from overseas motor and motorcycle manufacturers. This situation would change dramatically from the mid-1960s onwards, when there was a massive increase in imported foreign cars and motorcycles, especially from German, French, Swedish and Japanese manufacturers.

On the Isle of Wight the registration of new private motor vehicles increased steadily from 1953 onwards. Most of these vehicles were mass produced post-war models. Some of the most popular cars in the mid-1950s were the Morris Minor Series II, Austin A30, A40 and A50, the Ford Popular 103E, Prefect 100E, Consul Mk 1 and Zephyr Mk 1 and the Vauxhall Velox and Wyvern. There were also many other makes of British cars available and most of their models were sold to Isle of Wight businesses and residents in smaller numbers.

Many Isle of Wight garages had formal dealer or agent agreements with specific motor manufacturers for the sale, service and repair of their vehicles and the sale of accessories. In Newport Frank Cheverton Ltd. in Lower St. James Street was the main dealer on the Island for Ford and Austin cars and Fordson tractors. Canning Day Ltd. in South Street was the main dealer for Vauxhall cars plus Bedford commercial vehicles and coaches, while Fowlers Ltd. in Pyle Street was an important dealer for Morris cars and commercial vehicles. In addition Borough Hall Garage in the High Street supplied Rootes Group cars and various motorcycles. C.F. Stagg in South Street was another important supplier of motorcycles.

Some other major garages in the 1950s were Downing and Donovan's Ryde Garage which had a Standard and Triumph dealership, Esplanade Garage of Ryde (Ford), Wight Motors of Ryde, Westridge Filling Station, H.J. Aedy of Wootton and East Cowes, Davies of Shanklin, P.S. Harwood of Wootton, P.J. Duff of Sandown, Sandown Garage (Jowett), J.B. Eames of Sandown, G.K. Nash of Ventnor (Morris and Citroen), E.H. Crinage and Son of Ventnor, Millmore of Ventnor, Holmes of Cowes, Wadham Brothers (Northwood and Shanklin), P.V. Pritchett Ltd. (Hunnyhill Garage), Fairlee Garage (Newport), Totland Service Station and Hodge and Childs of Bembridge. There were many more garages and petrol filling stations in the smaller towns and villages. Some of these sold small numbers of new cars but they tended to concentrate more on vehicle servicing and repairs and the sale of second hand vehicles.

In February 1956 the branch railway from Newport to Sandown via Newchurch and Alverstone was closed by British Railways. By June 1956 Southern Vectis had achieved a virtual monopoly of local bus services on the Isle of Wight, the sole exception being Seaview Services Ltd.'s long established route from Ryde to Seaview via Puckpool. This short and busy route was operated by a pair of Leyland 'Titan' PD2/1A double deck buses GDL 764 and GDL 765 which were new to the operator in 1950. The mid and late 1950s continued to be a very successful period for the Island's many coach operators and they invested in large numbers of the latest vehicles to cope with the heavy demands for excursions, especially round-the-Island tours, during the summer months. Shotters Ltd., Moss Motor Tours (Sandown IW) Ltd., Southern Vectis, Fountain Coaches, E.H. Crinage and Son of Ventnor and West Wight Motor Bus Company Ltd. were some of the largest coach operators during this period. The 41-seat Bedford SB with Duple bodywork was the most popular new vehicle. Several other makes and models of coach were purchased, including Bristol LS, Commer Avenger and AEC Reliance vehicles.

4,360 new motor vehicles were registered on the Isle of Wight between January 1953 and December 1956, at an average annual rate of 1,090 per year. Registration numbers started at JDL 547 and ran through to NDL 906 in December 1956. It is known that 57 of these vehicles were buses, all of which were purchased by Southern Vectis. 47 of these buses were double deck Bristol Lodekkas and they provided much needed additional capacity following the early railway branch line closures. These Lodekkas were numbered as JDL 996 to JDL 999, KDL 1, KDL 401 to KDL 416, LDL 720 to LDL 739 and MDL 951 to MDL 956. 45 new coaches were purchased by 11 coach operators during this period, mainly by Moss Motor Tours Ltd., Shotters Ltd. and Southern Vectis. All of these new buses and coaches were issued with DL registrations.

In the following four years an additional 6,756 new Isle of Wight registrations were issued, at an average annual rate of 1,690 per year. Finally, a further 5,857 new 'DL' registrations were issued between January 1961 and February 1964. Registration numbers started at VDL 664 and ran through to YDL 999, then 1 ADL to 999 ADL, 1 BDL to 999 BDL and 1 CDL to around 500 CDL between November 1962 and February 1964. During this period the average annual rate of new registrations increased to 1,900 per year.

In the late 1950s British car manufacturers introduced many new and revised models. Morris produced huge numbers of its popular Minor 1000 with a single windscreen and a larger rear window. Austin introduced its A35 and A55 models, which were updated versions of the A30 and A50 with more powerful engines, modified bodywork and flashing indicators. Some other new models were the Vauxhall Victor and Cresta, the Austin A40 Farina, the Ford Zephyr and Zodiac Mk 2's and the Austin and Morris Minis. Large numbers of all of these cars were sold on the Island and were issued with DL registrations.

Around 1960 several radically different new models were introduced. Ford launched its Anglia 105E, Cortina Mk 1 and restyled Zephyr and Zodiac Mk 3 cars while Vauxhall produced its completely new Victor model. Most other manufacturers followed suit. Some companies (e.g. Jaguar) promoted revolutionary new sports car designs such as the iconic E-type while other companies (e.g. Morgan) preferred a more evolutionary approach. The Rootes Group introduced the Hillman Imp, a small mass produced rear-engined car, in competition with the Mini. Unfortunately this model was beset with initial faults and production problems at the troubled Linwood factory in Scotland. The Imp's commercial failure contributed to the eventual sale of the company to Chrysler in the mid-1960s.

There were many dairy farms on the Isle of Wight in the 1950s and 1960s. In those days there were very limited facilities for the refrigerated storage and transport of milk and the daily collection of fresh milk was essential. This was managed by specialist haulage firms who carried milk in churns from the farm entrances to the Island Dairies processing plant at the bottom of Lower St James Street in Newport. The largest such firm on the Island was P.R. Buckingham Ltd. of Newport. Buckingham's garage was located in Clifford Street near Drill Hall Road and it was equipped with its own private petrol tank and pump.

Islander Terry Knight remembers that his father was employed as a full time driver by Buckingham's in the early 1960s. The firm operated between six and ten DL-registered Morris lorries and each driver had several daily milk collection rounds. Terry's father had three rounds. The first covered the Whitecroft and Gatcombe area. The second covered Newport (Forest Road), Thorness, Porchfield, Newtown and Shalfleet while the third involved collections in East Cowes, Whippingham, Wootton and Fernhill. The traditional method of milk collection was changed to tanker lorries in the 1960s and 1970s. Buckingham's moved their garage to Westminster Lane, Newport around 1968 and later sold the business to the national company Wincanton. Terry Knight recalls that four members of staff had the same forename – Ron Knight, Ron Flux, Ron Drayton and Ron Johnson. This led to much light-hearted banter when these colleagues were in the depot at the same time.

During the period 1952 to 1964 no IDL, QDL or ZDL registrations were issued. This was national standard practice, to avoid possible confusion between letters and numbers with similar appearances. From February 1964 the Isle of Wight adopted the new national numbering system with year suffix letters (ADL 1B onwards). No registration numbers with the 1963 suffix letter A were issued on the Isle of Wight. All vehicles registered after February 1964 fall outside the remit of the present book. For the record some unused reversed CDL registration numbers continued to be issued slowly up to July 1976 alongside the new registration numbers with year suffix letters. These were issued for a variety of special reasons (e.g. re-registrations and retentions) and include the intriguing allocation of 523 CDL to 'Lucan' of London W1 on 7/4/1964 to replace a previous registration (XJJ 500).

The final part of this chapter contains photographs of a cross-section of DL-registered vehicles which were new between January 1953 and February 1964. As in chapters 1 and 2 the pictures have been arranged chronologically by their registration number (i.e. the date when they were first registered by the Isle of Wight County Council). Some of the vehicles will probably be familiar to most readers but a few of them were quite rare. Taken together it is hoped that these images will demonstrate the wide range of models which were in active use on Island roads fifty to sixty years ago. Hopefully the photographs will also provide clear evidence as to how British motor vehicle design changed during the early post-war period which is still within many people's living memory.

PHOTO GALLERY (1953 – 1964)

JDL 606 *was first registered on 17/1/1953. It was supplied by Fowler's Ltd., the Isle of Wight's main Morris dealer and its first owner was a Mr Dubs of Cowes. This car was one of many Morris Minor cars, estate cars and vans to be sold on the Island between 1949 and 1972. This is a Minor Series II which was produced with a distinctive split windscreen. The Morris Minor was a very successful British car and over 1.3 million units were made. There were three versions – the Minor MM (from 1948 to 1953), the Minor Series II (from 1952 to 1956) and the Minor 1000 (from 1956 to 1972). JDL 606 has been owned on the Island for many years by Colin Thomas. It is in excellent condition. (Colin Thomas)*

JDL 760 *was one of a batch of Bristol LS6B coaches with 39-seat Eastern Coachworks bodies that were supplied to Southern Vectis in 1953/54. Numbered JDL 757 to JDL 762 these vehicles formed a major part of the company's fleet of coaches until they were sold in 1968/69. (Author's collection)*

KDL 66 *was a Bedford Dormobile which was quite a popular vehicle in the mid-1950s for self-catering family touring holidays. This vehicle was first registered on 28/8/1953. It was supplied by Canning Day Ltd. and its first owner was a Mr Warder of Newchurch. The photograph was taken in Gurnard in the mid-1970s. (Peter Relf)*

KDL 104 *is a Ford Zephyr Six Mk 1 with a remarkable history. The 6-cylinder car with 2262cc engine still exists on the Island and is in excellent condition. KDL 104 was first registered on 11/9/1953. The car was supplied by Frank Cheverton Ltd. and its first owner was William "John" Snellgrove, a Newport businessman and keen rally driver. In November 1953 John Snellgrove entered KDL 104 in the Daily Express National Motor Rally. The Rally started in Plymouth and finished in Hastings via Hardwick, south of Edinbugh. KDL 104 completed the event. This was followed in April 1954 by the Isle of Wight Car Rally where John Snellgrove won the Concours d'Elegance prize in KDL 104. After this Mr Snellgrove undertook a continental journey of 2,382 miles in a fortnight – passing through Le Havre, Lyons, Grenoble, Pisa, Milan, Como, St. Gothard Pass, Interlaken, Berne, Geneva, Paris and back to Le Havre and home. Then in November 1954 KDL 104 was entered in the MCC Redex National Motor Rally where John Snellgrove achieved the distinction of being the class winner for 1300cc to 2600cc closed saloons. KDL 104's final competitive event was the Thames Estuary Auto Club's National "Cats' Eyes" Night Rally in February 1955. Unfortunately John Snellgrove was forced to retire with navigational problems. (Author)*

KDL 104 was sold off the Island in December 1957 to a Mr Wilfred Ashley in Hitchin, Hertfordshire, where it remained for 48 years. The Zephyr Six was restored in this period and used sparingly. When Mr Ashley passed away the car was sold again, this time moving to Minehead. A year later KDL 104 made an appearance on eBay and its current owner Martin Wallis was fortunate to purchase the car and return it to the Island. With the help of John Snellgrove's son, Philip, Martin Wallis has been able to trace much of the vehicle's history. In Martin Wallis' ownership KDL 104 has had full brake overhaul, all bushes replaced with superflex replacements, new Michelin XZX radial tyres, correct Mk 1 Borg Warner overdrive and new exhaust system fitted. Amazingly, the car has also been refitted with the original spotlights that were removed from the car in 1957. KDL 104 attends several classic car shows on the Island and mainland every year and unsurprisingly always attracts a lot of interest. (Philip Snellgrove collection)

KDL 142 *was another Ford Zephyr Six Mk 1 which was first registered on 24/9/1953. It was supplied by Esplanade Garage, Ryde to Mr Dorley Brown who lived in Ryde. This lovely colour period photograph was taken in High Park Road, Ryde and is believed to show Mrs Dorley Brown with the family car. (Internet/ Martin Wallis collection)*

KDL 152 *was a BSA Bantam 125cc motorcycle. It was supplied by the Kellaway motorcycle business in Ryde and was first registered on 1/10/1953. Over 400,000 BSA Bantams were sold between 1948 and 1971. The early models had a 125cc engine. Later models were built with a 150cc or 175cc engine. Many bright red Bantams were purchased by the GPO and used as telegram delivery bikes. (John Gregory collection)*

KDL 445 *was a BSA M20 500cc motorcycle combination which was used by the Automobile Association as a breakdown support vehicle. It was first registered on 19/1/1954 and was supplied by Stagg Motors of South Street, Newport. (Colin Thomas collection)*

KDL 301 *is a Ford Popular 103E with an 1172cc sidevalve engine, over 155,000 of which were manufactured between 1953 and 1959. When it was first produced the Ford Popular was the cheapest new car in the UK, at a time when other new cars and good second hand vehicles were relatively scarce. This car was first registered on 26/11/1953. It was supplied by Frank Cheverton Ltd. and its first owner was a Miss Goodwin of Newport who was the Almoner at St. Mary's Hospital. In 1954 she bought a Ford Prefect 100E and sold the Popular to Mr Albert Warne of Alvington.*

Mr Warne owned KDL 301 for over 35 years and had the car serviced at Frank Cheverton Ltd.'s garage in Newport. In 1990 Mr Warne's son came to speak to the late Bob Stay who had been a senior motor engineer at Chevertons before founding Stag Lane Motors in the mid-1960s. Bob agreed to purchase the car which was totally original with a low mileage. The vehicle has been part of the Stay family's collection of vintage and classic motor vehicles since 1990. These three photos were taken at Bob Stay's home in June 2016. (Author)

KDL 539 was an elegant Jaguar Mark VII saloon. It was supplied by Downing and Donovan Ltd. (Ryde Garage) to a Mr Russell of Ryde. It was first registered on 3/3/1954. This luxurious Jaguar car with a 3442cc engine was produced between 1950 and 1954. It was the first Jaguar car to be offered with automatic transmission. (Philip Snellgrove collection)

KDL 683 was an Austin A40 Somerset van. It was first registered on 4/4/1954 and was supplied by Frank Cheverton Ltd. to a Mr Moody of Carisbrooke. The vehicle was subsequently sold to Mr Morris Denham who used it for his building business on the Island and to carry his family for social trips and holidays. (Colin Denham collection)

KDL 892 *is a graceful Alvis Grey Lady sports saloon, with a 6-cylinder three litre engine. This car was first registered on 25/6/1954. It was supplied by Wadham Brothers to Mr J.C.W. Gould who lived in Newport. The car still exists on the mainland and is believed to be available for private hire for weddings and other special occasions. (Author's collection)*

LDL 120 *was a Humber Hawk saloon. It was first registered on 14/9/1954. The car was supplied by Wight Motors Ltd. to Mr A. Ash of Ryde. This photograph was taken in Station Street, Ryde in March 1974. (Peter Relf)*

LDL 146 *is an unusual Cyclemaster 32cc micromotor. These machines enjoyed a few years of popularity in the UK in the mid-1950s. In 1953 there were over a dozen types of these clip-on engines for bicycles available. Micromotors were effectively superseded by mopeds in the late 1950s and 1960s. This vehicle was first registered on 23/9/1954. It was supplied by Smith and Whitehead to a Mr. Baker of Newport. This preserved Cyclemaster still exists on the Island and was photographed at Havenstreet in 2015. (Author)*

LDL 308 *is a Morris Commercial J-type minibus. It was first registered on 19/11/1954. This minibus was supplied by Wadham Brothers to a Mr Masler of Ryde. Morris Commercial J-type vehicles were normally built as vans and many were purchased by the GPO for the collection and delivery of mail, including parcels. It is believed that this vehicle was initially used by Bishop Lovett School as a minibus but was sold after about a year because it was too small for this purpose. Apart from one trip to the continent this vehicle has remained on the Isle of Wight. It is powered by a 1500cc side valve engine with a four speed gearbox. This vehicle was fitted with all the extras available in 1954 including a heater, a passenger side windscreen wiper and illuminated trafficator arm indicators. Very few J-type minibuses have survived but LDL 308 still exists on the Island and is in storage ready to be restored. This photograph was taken in Ryde High Street in June 1974. (Peter Relf)*

The **STANDARD** *Eight*

with 8 new plus features

LDL 673 *was a grey Standard Ten saloon. It was supplied by I and K Hooper to Mr Hooper who lived in Sandown. The car was first registered on 14/3/1955. The upper photograph shows a period advertisement for Standard Eight cars around the mid-1950s. (Colin Thomas collection). The lower photograph of LDL 673 was taken in Bullen Road, Ryde in May 1974. (Peter Relf)*

LDL 722 *was a Bristol LD6G double deck bus with Eastern Coachworks bodywork. This bus was one of 65 Bristol Lodekka buses to enter service with Southern Vectis between 1954 and 1959, partly for rail service replacement duties. All of these vehicles had DL registrations (JDL 996 – JDL 999, KDL 1, KDL 401 – KDL 406, LDL 720 – LDL 739, MDL 951 – MDL 956, ODL 7 – ODL 15, PDL 516 – PDL 519 and SDL 265 – SDL 269). This photograph of LDL 722 was taken in Godshill in the late 1950s. The bus was on its way from Newport to Sandown. (Copyright W.J. Nigh and Sons, Ltd., Shanklin, IW)*

LDL 815 *is a 1955 Ariel Square Four 1000cc motorcycle with a contemporary sidecar. It was pictured at the Mottistone transport show over the Easter weekend in 2017. This powerful motorcycle is in excellent condition with an Isle of Wight owner. (Colin Thomas)*

MDL 95 *is a Sunbeam Talbot Mk 3 saloon. It was first registered on 1/7/1955. The car was supplied by Wight Motors and its first owner was a Mr Hawksworth of Yarmouth. This car still exists in good running condition on the Isle of Wight. The lower photograph shows a rear view of MDL 95 on its way to the Easter 2017 Mottistone transport show. (Upper photo Martin Wallis collection; lower photo Maryrose Thomas)*

MDL 214 *was a black Ford Consul Mk I. The Consul was Ford's first 'new' post-war car when it was launched in 1951 and it contained several innovative design features. It was fitted with hydraulic brakes and had a single piece body shell (i.e. an integrated chassis and body). It was supplied by N. Baker Ltd. and was first registered on 25/7/1955. The first registered owner was Millership and Tompkins of Sandown. This photograph was taken in Marlborough Road, Ryde on 6/6/1974. (Peter Relf)*

This vibrant postcard photograph of Ryde Esplanade was taken around 1955. It shows a DL-registered Southern Vectis Lodekka double deck bus, several taxis and a number of private cars. This was a typical view of the town seen by thousands of families as they arrived for their Isle of Wight holidays each year. (Copyright W.J. Nigh and Sons, Ltd., Shanklin, IW)

Whitecliff Bay caravan park, near Bembridge, was one of several large holiday camps/ villages on the Isle of Wight. This postcard photograph provides a clear impression of the scale and the layout of the site and its close proximity to the beach. Bedford dormobile MDL 450 may be seen in the foreground. This vehicle was supplied by Canning Day Ltd. and was first registered on 1/10/1955. The first registered owner was a Mr Gladdis of Sandown. (Copyright W.J. Nigh and Sons Ltd., Shanklin, IW)

MDL 325 *was a black Rover 90 saloon. Borough Hall Garage supplied this car to a Mr Cooper of Newport. It was first registered on 30/8/1955. (Peter Relf)*

MDL 881 *was a Francis Barnett 197cc motorcycle. It was purchased new by Mr Dave Warne of Parkhurst. The supplier was Kellaway and the bike was first registered on 7/2/1956. The photograph shows a young Dave Warne on MDL 881 when it was probably almost new. (Dave Warne collection)*

MDL 867 is a Humber Hawk Mk VI saloon. It was supplied by Wight Motors Ltd. of Ryde and was first registered on 26/1/1956. This beautiful car was sold to local businessman Mr Harry Ross, who owned the vehicle for 4 years before trading it back to Wight Motors Ltd. The next owner was a Mr John Woodham, also of Ryde. He drove the car sparingly until he sadly passed away in 1980. Mr Woodham's widow and son kept the car garaged and maintained for the next 26 years but it was not used on the road. The Humber was recommissioned in 2006 and acquired by its present owner who lives on the Island. He has gradually restored the vehicle and sometimes displays it at local classic car shows. These two photographs were taken at Lake in February 2015. (Terry Jones)

MDL 888 is a legendary Austin Healey 100 sports car, designed by Donald Healey, and fitted with the same 2660cc engine which powered the Austin A90 Atlantic. This car was named the 100 because it was capable of achieving speeds of 100m.p.h. MDL 888 was first registered on the Isle of Wight on 3/2/1956. It was supplied by Frank Cheverton Ltd. to Mr Seabrooke of Newtown. This magnificent vehicle is currently owned by Shane Brading on the Island and it is in excellent condition. (Chris Wood collection)

NDL 318 *is a 1956 Series 1 Landrover. It was sold new to the late Mr Taylor of Hill Farm, Gatcombe and was first registered on 9/6/1956. The vehicle was supplied by Frank Cheverton Ltd. The Landrover was used by Mr Taylor around his farm until 1996 when it was laid up in a barn. In 2006 there was a dispersal sale and Colin Thomas became the second owner of NDL 318 on the Isle of Wight. (Colin Thomas)*

NDL 496 *was an incredibly rare Paramount roadster. This car was supplied by Totland Service Station to a Mr Broadbent of Totland. It was first registered on 26/7/1956. Paramount Cars was a British company which produced the Paramount automobile between 1950 and 1956. Initially the firm was based in Derbyshire. Originally it was intended that the car would have an Alvis engine and suspension but to reduce costs the production versions used Ford Ten components including the 1172cc side valve engine. The Paramount was built in both saloon and roadster form. In 1953 the company was bought by Camden Motors and moved to Leighton Buzzard and the Ford Consul 1508cc engine became an option in a longer chassis. Production ceased in 1956 when only around 75 cars had been made. Keith Brading, who built replica Austin Healey 'frogeye' Sprites on the Island between 1986 and 1998, remembers that NDL 496 was owned by a Sandown hotelier for some time and that it had its petrol tank in a side wing. The photograph was taken in south west London in July 1963 when the car was seven years old. (Nick Georgano)*

NDL 513 *is a Volkswagen Beetle. It was first registered on 1/8/1956. The car was supplied by Modern Light Cars and its first owner was a Mr Fisk of Shanklin. During the next 52 years the VW had three more owners, all of whom lived on the Isle of Wight. NDL 513 (known as Olive) has been owned by Nick Morter on the Island since 2008. He has carried out quite a lot of mechanical work, including engine overhaul, front steering/ suspension overhaul and renewal of brake system. Nick has replaced the bonnet and had a few small sections resprayed. This distinctive car is pretty much original. The photograph of Olive was taken in the Cowes front garden of the parents of one of Nick's friends. (Nick Morter)*

ODL 370 *was a light green single windscreen Morris Minor 1000. It was supplied by Harwood's garage to a Mr Clarke of Binstead and was first registered on 26/4/1957. Originally the car was fitted with semaphore indicators. This photograph was taken in Ryde in June 1974. (Peter Relf)*

ODL 777 *was a Humber Super Snipe. It was first registered on 25/7/1957. This fine car was supplied by Trigg Ltd. of Esher, Surrey. The first owner of ODL 777 was Mr Grimaldi of Ryde. The author remembers that these Humber cars were popular as taxis on the Island as a result of their large passenger and luggage carrying capacity. The photograph was taken in Ryde. (Peter Relf)*

PDL 108 *was a Morris Commercial ambulance. It was supplied by Wadham Brothers to J. Samuel White Ltd., Cowes and was first registered on 18/10/1957. When this photograph was taken at The Isle of Wight Steam Railway at Havenstreet in August 1982 the vehicle was owned by St. John Ambulance, Ryde. (Peter Relf)*

PDL 149 *is a Reliant three-wheeler. This small convertible car was first registered on 19/10/1957. It was supplied by P.V. Pritchett Ltd. (Hunnyhill garage) and its first owner was Mr F.J.G. Mills. PDL 149 still exists on the Isle of Wight. (Colin Thomas)*

PDL 641 *is a Series 1 Landrover. It was supplied by Wadhams Ltd. to Mr A.E. Brown who lived in Newport. The vehicle was first registered on 18/3/1958. When this photograph was taken in Victoria Street, Ryde in June 1974 the sturdy Landrover was being used as a recovery vehicle by Ryde Garage (Downing and Donovan). PDL 641 still exists on the Island and has been restored to near original condition. (Peter Relf)*

PDL 906 *was a blue Austin A35 with a 948cc engine. It was first registered on 15/5/1958 and its first owner was Mr Crow of Seaview. The car was supplied by Frank Cheverton Ltd. This photograph was taken in Lower Highland Road, Ryde in March 1981 when the car was over 22 years old. (Peter Relf)*

EDL 946, RDL 149, VDL 42 and YDL 168 *are Vauxhall cars and form part of Colin Thomas' superb collection of vintage and classic motor vehicles on the Isle of Wight, all of which have original DL registrations. RDL 149 is a Series 1 F-type Victor with 1500cc engine that was first registered on 1/7/1958. It was supplied by Harwood's garage to Della Crisp in Binstead. Mr Crisp sold the car to Colin Thomas in 1985. VDL 42 is a Cresta with a 2262cc 6-cylinder engine that was supplied by Canning Day Ltd. to a Mr Parsons of Shanklin. It was first registered on 25/7/1960. Colin bought the car in 1979 in unroadworthy condition.*

YDL 168 *is another PA Cresta. The car was built with the later 2651cc engine and the optional automatic gearbox. It was first registered on 25/5/1962 and its first owner was a Mr Henry Cook of Newport. Colin Thomas purchased this fine car from Aedy's garage in Wootton in 1983 when it had only 26,000 miles showing. Both the Victor RDL 149 and Cresta VDL 42 have required major restorations. The restoration of RDL 149 should be completed by 2018. All four cars are in very good condition and make regular appearances at various car shows on the Island. (Colin Thomas)*

PDL 611 *was a Bedford SB3 coach with Duple Vega C41F bodywork. It was supplied by Canning Day Ltd. and was first registered on 25/3/1958. The first registered owner was Randall and Sons of Ventnor and the coach was often used on round-the-Island tours in the late 1950s and early 1960s. Note the unusual twin tone air horn just above the driver's window. This vehicle was sold to Shamrock and Rambler (THC Ltd.), Cowes in July 1967. (Copyright W.J. Nigh and Sons Ltd., Shanklin, IW).*

RDL 863 *is a McCormick tractor. It was first registered on 5/12/1958 and its first owner was Mr Stallard who lived in the Shanklin area. The vehicle was supplied by Arthur Wood Ltd. This tractor still exists on the Island and is in very good condition. (Colin Thomas)*

SDL 979 *was a Ford Prefect 100E which was produced between 1953 and 1959. It was supplied by Frank Cheverton Ltd. to a Mr Morris who lived in Niton. The car was first registered on 6/7/1959. This photograph was taken at Arreton in August 1982. (Peter Relf)*

TDL 105 *is a Triumph Tigress motor scooter. This British motor scooter (later sold as the BSA Sunbeam) was made with a 175cc or 250cc engine. It was first registered on 21/7/1959. Borough Hall Garage supplied TDL 105 to its first owner, a Mr Woodmore of Cowes. This vehicle still exists on the Isle of Wight and is in good running condition. The photograph was taken at a gathering of classic motor vehicles at Sandown Airport in 2015. (Martin Wallis)*

TDL 189 *was a large coal delivery lorry belonging to George Weeks and Son. It was first registered on 7/8/1959 to Weeks and Son of Calbourne and was supplied by George Weeks. In this atmospheric photograph the lorry is seen negotiating deep snow in a narrow country lane, probably during the very harsh winter of 1962/63 when heavy snowfalls remained unmelted for almost two months. (Keir Foss collection)*

TDL 345 *was a Hillman Minx III saloon. Wight Motors Ltd. supplied this car to a Mr Jaeger of Sandown. It was first registered on 17/9/1959. TDL 345 was pictured in the George Street car park, Ryde in April 1983. (Peter Relf)*

TDL 723 *was one of many Vauxhall Victors to be sold on the Island. Most of these cars, including TDL 723, were supplied by Canning Day Ltd. in Newport. The car was first registered on 10/12/1959 and its first owner was a Mr Ayers of Totland Bay. This photograph was taken at St Helens Duver in April 1983. (Peter Relf)*

TDL 728 *was an Austin Healey 'frogeye' Sprite. It was first registered on 11/12/1959. The sports car was supplied by F.H. Winter and Son to a Mr Cavanagh of Havenstreet. In the late 1960s TDL 728 was owned by David White who provided these two period photographs. David has owned several vintage and classic cars on the Island over the past forty years, including an extremely rare Hudson Terraplane roadster. (David White collection)*

UDL 853 *was a large Morris lorry. It was first registered in 1960 to P.R. Buckingham Ltd. of Newport. This lorry was one of around eight large DL-registered Morris lorries in Buckingham's fleet of milk collection vehicles, when fresh milk needed to be collected daily from all Isle of Wight dairy farms. The lower photograph shows UDL 853 and four of the other Buckingham lorries. These would have been a very familiar sight on Island roads and country lanes in the 1950s and 1960s. (Terry Knight collection)*

VDL 634 *is a rare and stylish Triumph Herald convertible. This car was supplied by Downing and Donovan Ltd. (Ryde Garage) to a Mr Green of Ventnor. It was first registered on 8/12/1960. VDL 634 is currently owned on the mainland by Triumph Herald convertible enthusiast Nick Price. He has researched the detailed history of the car. Upon first launch in March 1960 all the convertibles were destined for overseas, with most being exported to the USA, Canada, South Africa and Australia. The car was the first Herald convertible on the Island. She came from the Standard Triumph distributor Munn and Underwood in Southsea and was on display at Ryde Garage from 25th August 1960. Curiously the car was made ready for sale in 1961 by H.J. Aedy to her 'first owner', a Mr Stimson of Colwell. She replaced a Bond minicar and spent the next 23 years based in the West Wight, never leaving the Island. Mr and Mrs Stimson had the car serviced regularly at Totland Service Station, The Broadway, Totland (Morris dealers).*

The Stimsons finally sold VDL 634 in 1984 when they traded the car in for a Volkswagen. The vehicle was then sold to a new owner in Herne Bay, Kent. In the early 2000s she appeared on the front cover of 'Practical Classics' magazine. VDL 634 remains unrestored and is the most original, early Herald convertible left in the UK. For further information on this special car please visit www.triumphheraldconvertible.co.uk. (Nick Price)

convertible MAGIC!

Here is all the world-famous magic of the Triumph Herald in Convertible form . . . a lithe, open-air roadster that gives you saloon car protection against wind and rain. The new Triumph Herald Convertible has all the unique Triumph Herald features—four wheel independent suspension, no greasing points, tail chasing turning circle, and a host of others— and the lively, economical twin-carburettor version of the famous 948 c.c. engine. **£766. 2. 6 Inc. P.T.**

STANDARD — TRIUMPH

The NEW
TRIUMPH HERALD
CONVERTIBLE

SEE IT, TRY IT, BUY IT AT

DOWNING & DONOVAN

Standard Main Agents

RYDE GARAGE, VICTORIA STREET, RYDE. Tel. 2043

VDL 880 is a Vauxhall Cresta. It was first registered on 14/2/1961. Canning Day Ltd. supplied the car and its first owner was a Mr Parsons of Ryde. The car is currently owned by Eddie James on the Isle of Wight and it may sometimes be seen at local classic car shows. VDL 880 was on display at the Vectis Historic Vehicle Club's Open Day at Arreton Barns in June 2016. The photographer's 1966 Sunbeam Tiger may be seen at the rear of the picture.

(Jeremy Chessell)

(The 1960 Vauxhall advertisement above is from Colin Thomas' collection)

The new 1961 **VAUXHALLS**

Victor
Velox
Cresta

built for the Motorway age

VDL 846 *was a blue Ford Anglia 105E. The completely redesigned Anglia with a 997cc or 1198cc engine was a very popular small family car, with just over 1 million units sold between 1959 and 1967. It was supplied by P.S. Harwood (Lushington Hill Garage) to the garage showroom and was first registered on 3/2/1961. The car was photographed in Prince Street, Ryde. (Peter Relf)*

VDL 966 *was a Bedford TJ lorry. It was supplied by Canning Day Ltd. to Mr Harold Biles (1898 – 1961). The lorry was first registered on 1/3/1961. It was used by the Biles' long-established family business for dealing and transporting livestock and collecting and disposing of fallen stock from Island farms. The lorry was based at Park Green Farm, Forest Road, Newport. Leaning against the lorry is David Biles (1935 – 2015) and just behind him is Ken Hunnybun in the white coat. The photograph was taken at the IW Agricultural Society's Annual Show at Blackwater in 1962 or 1963. (Sam Biles collection)*

WDL 220 *was a Bedford SB1 coach with Duple Super Vega C41F body. It was supplied to Seaview Services Ltd. by Canning Day Ltd. and was first registered on 3/5/1961. The Bedford SB coach was the sleek successor to the Bedford OB. It proved to be extremely popular and became the backbone of many Isle of Wight coach operators' fleets in the 1950s and early 1960s. WDL was photographed at Ryde Esplanade coach park in 1978. (Peter Relf)*

WDL 632 *is a British-built BMW Isetta bubblecar with a 298cc engine. This microcar was supplied by S.G.T. Williams (Esso Service Station) to a Mr Holman of Gurnard. It was first registered on 1/7/1961. The Isetta was one of several makes of small three-wheeled vehicles in the 1950s and 1960s (others included Berkeley, Bond, Heinkel and Messerschmitt) which were quite numerous for several years. WDL 632 was photographed at the Havenstreet Classic Car Show in June 2001. The picture alongside of a 1950s Heinkel bubblecar from the author's collection shows how the vehicle was accessed through its front door. (Martin Wallis)*

WDL 691 *is a Hillman Husky van. It was supplied by Sandford Garage, Godshill to itself and was first registered on 7/7/1961. This vehicle probably still exists on the Island. The photograph was taken at the Butterfly World Classic Car Show in 2003. (Colin Thomas)*

WDL 864 *is a Triumph 3TA 350cc motorcycle. It was first registered on 25/7/1961. The motorcycle was supplied by Kellaway to a Mr Rickman of Freshwater. WDL 864 was photographed at Brading in 2012 when the bike was owned by a Mr Truman. (Martin Wallis)*

XDL 228 *is a Jaguar Mark 2 saloon. This high performing 6-cylinder car was fitted with a 2.4, 3.4 or 3.8 litre engine. XDL 228 was first registered on 23/10/1961. It was supplied by P.S. Harwood Ltd. (Wootton) to a Mr Morris of Newport. XDL 228 still exists and was seen for sale at Beaulieu recently. In this action picture the Jaguar Mark 2 is seen driving past a pair of stationary coaches at Ryde Esplanade. (Peter Relf)*

XDL 559 *is a preserved Bedford fire engine. This emergency vehicle was supplied by Isle of Wight County Council to the IWCC Fire Service. It was first registered on 24/4/1962. XDL 559 was pictured in Freshwater in March 2003 immediately prior to taking a bride to her wedding. (Peter Relf/ Vectamart)*

XDL 606 was a Vauxhall VX4/90 saloon. The car was supplied by Canning Day Ltd. to their garage, presumably for sale through their Newport showroom. It was first registered on 2/2/1962. This photograph was taken in Broadway Crescent, Pell Estate, Ryde in May 1974. (Peter Relf)

XDL 904 was a Triumph Herald saloon. The car was supplied by the Standard and Triumph dealer Downing and Donovan Ltd. to a Mr Boyd of Yarmouth. It was first registered on 12/4/1962. XDL 904 was pictured in Seaview in August 1983 when it was over 20 years old. (Peter Relf)

YDL 123 *was a Singer Vogue saloon. The car was first registered on 16/5/1962. It was supplied by P.S. Harwood Ltd. to a Mr Holt of Newport. This photograph of YDL 123 was taken in Bettesworth Road, Ryde in August 1982. (Peter Relf)*

YDL 442 *is an Austin Mini Seven saloon with 848cc engine which still exists on the Isle of Wight. This car was built in September 1961 and sold by St John's Road Garage, Ryde to its first owner Arthur Shotter of Brighstone on 11th July 1962. Mr Shotter owned the car for 18 years. It then changed hands three times by 1992 and was in a state of disrepair. The saviour of the car was David Perkis of Staddlestones Garage and St. John's Garage, Ryde MOT Station. David stored the car for 14 years before he was persuaded to sell it for restoration to Adrian Eldridge of Niton. With assistance from well-known Mini expert Simon Darby the car was stripped bare and mounted horizontally on a scaffold pole to act as a rotissary. Following months of work and complete restoration all rust was eradicated and a new sub frame installed. YDL 442 is now owned by Peter Hodgson, the Chairman of the Vectis Historic Vehicle Club. Regular maintenance and further cosmetic improvements keep the car looking good. The interior is still as original from 1961. (Author)*

YDL 454 *is a Vauxhall Victor saloon. This attractive car still exists on the Island and is in superb condition. It has been owned by the same family since it was first registered on 12/7/1962. The car was supplied by P.S. Harwood Ltd. to Mr Flux in Shanklin. YDL 454 has been owned and maintained by Mr Flux's son Nigel for many years. Nigel Flux takes his Vauxhall Victor to several classic car shows on the Island each year. The above photograph was taken at the VHVC Open Day at Arreton Barns in June 2016. (Author)*

YDL 457 *was a Sunbeam Alpine roadster. This sports car was supplied by Wight Motors Ltd. to its first owner, a Mr McClelland of Sandown. The car was first registered on 13/7/1962. The photograph was taken at The Parade, Cowes during the 1995 Cowes Classic Car Event. It is not known if this car still exists. (Martin Wallis)*

YDL 843 *was a Lambretta LI 150cc motor scooter which may still exist. It was first registered on 5/10/1962. The motor scooter was supplied by Borough Hall Garage (Motorcycles Dept.) to a Mr Wickens of Niton. This photograph of Lambretta YDL 843 was taken in East Cowes in June 2001. (Martin Wallis)*

YDL 882 *was a maroon Ford Zephyr Mark 3. The 6-cylinder car was supplied by Frank Cheverton Ltd. and its first owner was a Mr Sutherland of Ryde. YDL 882 was photographed in Victoria Street, Ryde in June 1974. (Peter Relf)*

YDL 961 *was an Austin Mini. It was first registered on 1/11/1962. Frank Cheverton Ltd. supplied the car and its first owner was a Mr Bower of Cowes. The period photo was probably taken in the early 1960s, possibly just after YDL 961 was purchased. The identity of the woman standing at the side of the Mini is unknown. (Author's collection)*

55 ADL *was a late Ford Popular 100E. It was first registered on 22/11/1962. Supplied by Norman Baker Ltd. this car's first owner was a Mr Wagner of Sandown. The 1950s design of this car made it appear rather old fashioned in the early 1960s alongside the Ford Cortina and Anglia 105E models. 55 ADL was pictured in Seaview in June 1974. (Peter Relf)*

278 ADL *was a Vauxhall Victor saloon. Canning Day Ltd. supplied this car to a Mr Marvin of Cowes and it was first registered on 10/1/1963. The photograph was taken outside the former Marine Court, The Parade, Cowes, probably around 1964. (Copyright W.J. Nigh and Sons Ltd., Shanklin, IW)*

462 ADL *was one of a batch of eight Bristol SUL4A single deck buses with 36-seat Eastern Coachworks bodies. These buses were new to Southern Vectis in 1963 and were numbered consecutively from 458 ADL to 465 ADL. They were sold in 1975 after just 12 years' service. 462 ADL was photographed at a busy Newport bus station. Also in the picture are two more Bristol SUL4As – 458 ADL and 461 ADL. (Peter Relf)*

806 ADL was a Morris Mini Traveller. This car was first registered on 11/4/1963. It was supplied by H.J. Aedy and its first owner was Gould, Hibberd and Randall Ltd. of Newport. Later in the 1960s 806 ADL became Norman Fallick's car and he owned it for a number of years. Norman recalls driving it for several long distance family holidays. (Norman Fallick collection)

843 ADL is a Morris Minor 1000 Traveller. This wood-framed estate version provided a large amount of additional space for carrying pets and luggage. 843 ADL was first registered on 19/4/1963. It was supplied by Binstead Garage Ltd to a Mr Cook of Ryde. The estate car was pictured at a recent classic car show at Havenstreet. (Colin Thomas)

910 ADL *was a Bedford VAS1 coach which was delivered new to Shotters Ltd. in May 1963. This compact vehicle had a Duple Bella Vista 29-seat body. It was used for a range of excursion and private hire duties including the carriage of escorted prisoners to and from the Island. The coach was sold to Scarlets Coaches of Minehead in April 1974. (Peter Relf)*

343 BDL *is an unusual Morris Commercial with camper van body. This vehicle was first registered on 28/6/1963. It was supplied by H.J. Aedy to a Mr Peach of Sandown. This vehicle still exists on the Isle of Wight. (Colin Thomas)*

776 BDL *was an MG 1100 saloon. This car was supplied by H.J. Aedy to a Mr Cross of Newport. It was first registered on 11/9/1963. The vehicle was later sold to Dr Mike Howell, who is the current Chairman of the Isle of Wight Austins group. 776 BDL is shown in the picture on the left (c. 1970) with Mike Howell's two children who are now mature adults. (Mike Howell collection)*

935 BDL *was a light blue Morris Mini saloon. It was supplied by H.J. Aedy to its first owner Mr Merrill of Binstead. The car was first registered on 4/10/1963. This photograph was taken in High Park Road, Ryde in September 1981. (Peter Relf)*

480 CDL *was an Austin Cambridge. This car was supplied by Marshall's Garage to a Mr Horton of Ryde. It was first registered on 15/1/1964 and was one of the last new motor vehicles to be issued with a reversed CDL number before the year suffix registrations came into effect in February 1964. The photo was taken in Ryde Road, Seaview. (Peter Relf)*

499 CDL *was a Ford Zodiac Mark II. According to the original IWCC vehicle registration register this vehicle was supplied by Mr Boynton in Sandown to himself on 18/3/1964. There is a reference that this vehicle was previously registered as GB 211. The photograph was taken in Brading in April 1985. (Peter Relf)*

555 CDL *was a grey Wolseley 1600. It was first registered on 1/6/1965. H.J. Aedy supplied this car to a Mr White in Ningwood. 555 CDL was photographed in Circular Road, Elmfield, Ryde in August 1983. This 1965 registration suggests that the Isle of Wight County Council may have issued a few reversed CDL numbers for new motor vehicles in parallel with the year suffix numbers which were allocated from February 1964 onwards. (Peter Relf)*

Appendix 1 – Registration numbers issued by Isle of Wight County Council

DL 1 – DL 9999	December 1903 to October 1935
ADL 1 – ADL 999	October 1935 to January 1937
BDL 1 – BDL 999	January 1937 to April 1938
CDL 1 – CDL 999	April 1938 to September 1939
DDL 1 – DDL 999	September 1939 to March 1946
EDL 1 – EDL 999	March 1946 to July 1947
FDL 1 – FDL 999	July 1947 to March 1949
GDL 1 – GDL 999	March 1949 to August 1950
HDL 1 – HDL 999	August 1950 to March 1952
JDL 1 – JDL 999	March 1952 to July 1953
KDL 1 – KDL 999	July 1953 to July 1954
LDL 1 – LDL 999	July 1954 to May 1955
MDL 1 – MDL 999	May 1955 to March 1956
NDL 1 – NDL 999	March 1956 to January 1957
ODL 1 – ODL 999	January 1957 to September 1957
PDL 1 – PDL 999	September 1957 to May 1958
RDL 1 – RDL 999	May 1958 to January 1959
SDL 1 – SDL 999	January 1959 to July 1959
TDL 1 – TDL 999	July 1959 to February 1960
UDL 1 – UDL 999	February 1960 to July 1960
VDL 1 – VDL 999	July 1960 to March 1961
WDL 1 – WDL 999	March 1961 to August 1961
XDL 1 – XDL 999	August 1961 to April 1962
YDL 1 – YDL 999	April 1962 to November 1962
1 ADL – 999 ADL	November 1962 to May 1963
1 BDL – 999 BDL	May 1963 to October 1963
1 CDL – 522 CDL	October 1963 to February 1964
ADL 1B onwards	February 1964 onwards

n.b. The registration numbers 523 CDL – 862 CDL were issued gradually between April 1964 and July 1976 to accommodate 'retentions' and 'transfers' of earlier DL registrations.

Appendix 2 – Some examples of Isle of Wight garages

*Internal view of Chevertons'
Ford workshop, 1952
(Barry Price collection)*

Frank Cheverton Ltd., Lugley Street Newport was the largest garage on the Isle of Wight throughout the 1940s, 1950s and 1960s and was the main dealer for Ford, Fordson, Austin and Rover vehicles. This family business was founded in 1852 as a coachbuilding and repair firm by Frank Cheverton's grandfather William at Broadlands, Newport. In 1872 William Cheverton died and the business was carried on by his two sons, with Mr R. Bird Cheverton as manager. Chevertons soon became well known for their high quality carriages and they were commissioned to make 17 horse-drawn vehicles for Queen Victoria.

Mr R. Bird Cheverton had six sons who were engaged in the business. One of these sons, Frank, entered the business in 1897. He spent several years on the mainland learning the motor trade with the Progress Motor Co. at Coventry. In 1905 Frank Cheverton returned to the Island and opened a motor department in Lugley Street. The whole business was sold in 1923 and Frank bought the Ford and Tractor part of the company together with approximately one third of the premises at Lugley Street. A few years later he purchased the remaining two thirds of the original premises and went on to acquire additional premises at Coppins Bridge. From the 1930s onwards Frank Cheverton Ltd. steadily expanded its car, van, truck and tractor sales plus its vehicle servicing and repairs. The firm also provided extensive bodybuilding and painting services and developed a major self-drive car hire department. 105 staff were employed and 16 service vans, trucks and breakdown vehicles were operated by Chevertons during their centenary in 1952. Frank Cheverton Ltd. continued to flourish up to the 1980s when the business was sold to Premier Motors.

"*The garage was cold, unheated, damp, dirty, unlit and badly equipped but with a set of hand tools it had a friendly atmosphere almost never to be found since (in my career). The garage had many loyal friends and customers and gave a service equal to any other of that day. We worked long hours. I remember that I had only three half days in one year and finishing at four was considered a half day. My wages at 14 were ten shillings a week, at 15 twelve shillings and six pence and at 16 fifteen shillings.*

We had many types of cars and lorries to service, mostly 1930 to 1940 models. There were no service exchange parts in those days and dynamos, starters, petrol pumps, radiators, engines, etc. all had to be serviced by ourselves. Tyres did not last very long being poor quality so these were always needing to be fitted, when you could get them because of the shortage, and punctures to be repaired. There was no minimum tread depth either and many people ran their tyres right down to the canvas.

A lot of cars were laid up at the garage for the duration of the war because only vital war workers were allowed petrol. Even then it was rationed. There was in fact only one petrol station open in Newport. That was Canning Days at the junction of South Street and Church Litten where Morrisons is currently located. There was no branded petrol. It was just known as 'Pool' and the pumps were painted grey.

Borough Hall garage, 18A High Street, Newport (adjacent to the current Hogshead public house) sold and serviced cars and motorcycles. It was the main dealer for the Rootes Group (Hillman, Humber, Singer, Sunbeam, Talbot, Commer and Karrier) in the 1940s and 1950s. After many years in Newport the business moved to East Cowes. This internal photograph was probably taken in 1949 and shows Norman Fallick in front of Hillman Minx FDL 909. The car was first registered on 18th January 1949 and its first owner was a Mr Cole of Newport, who supplied the car to himself.

Norman Fallick's memories of Borough Hall Garage, Newport during the war

Norman Fallick has lived in Newport for virtually all of his life. Born in 1928 Norman developed an early interest in motor vehicles. After leaving school in 1942 his first full time job was to be employed as a boy at Borough Hall Garage at 18A High Street, almost opposite County Hall. The following extracts from Norman's unpublished life story provide a fascinating insight into how an Isle of Wight garage operated during the war.

Most of the cars laid up belonged to residents and customers who lived nearby. Some I remember were:

Mr Bullock	builder	Willys Overland Whippet
Mr Norman	music shop	Morris Eight
Mr Raynor	engineer	M.G.
Mr Bowley	Armed Forces	Ford Eight
Mr Jolliffe	pie shop	Vauxhall Fourteen
Mr Russell	garage owner	Standard Twelve
Mr Cool	solicitor	Hillman Minx
Miss Marder	clothes shop	Austin Sixteen
Mr Spanner	clothes shop	Standard Ten
	Victory Cleaners	Ford Eight van

Borough Hall Garage also had a Motorcycle Department and had quite a number of bikes laid up as well. Some I remember were a Brough Superior, Vincent HRD, an old Royal Enfield with a square petrol tank, plus an assortment of Norton, BSA, Triumph, AJS, Matchless and an Ariel Square Four. Sometimes we did other jobs. On one occasion I went with another mechanic to bring back to life an old single cylinder stationary engine in a barn at Arreton. We also serviced boats at Newtown."

This photograph shows Borough Hall Garage motor engineer Norman Fallick at the wheel of his first car, an MG PA roadster, registration number TJ 4060. The picture was taken at Carisbrooke Castle around 1952.

Canning Day Ltd., South Street, Newport was a major Island business and was of similar importance to Frank Cheverton Ltd. in the 1940s and 1950s. The firm had several premises in South Street, including the garage and petrol filling station on the corner of Church Litten which is now part of the Morrisons supermarket site. This garage was formerly owned by Smith and Whitehead (see photo below). Canning Day Ltd. was the main Vauxhall and Bedford dealer for the Island and was a key supplier of buses, coaches and commercial vehicles to local businesses. During the Second World War the garage had a strategic role in the supply of scarce new vans, lorries and buses and was the only supplier of petrol in Newport when fuel for civilian use was being rationed.

(Barry Price collection)

Fowler's Ltd., Pyle Street, Newport was another important garage located in the heart of Newport. It was the main Morris dealer for the Island and supplied and serviced many Morris cars, vans and lorries. Fowler's Ltd. also sold petrol from its forecourt. The two photographs on this page show an external and internal view of the firm's premises in the 1950s.

(Isle of Wight County Record Office)

External and internal views of the Downing and Donovan Ltd. garage, Ryde c. 1955. Both pictures include Mr de Castel-Branco's Triumph Renown GDL 107.

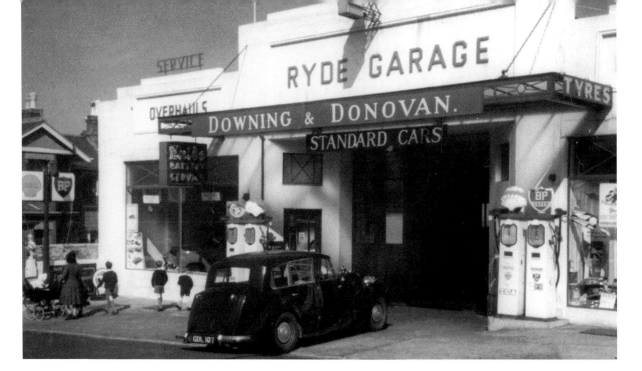

Downing and Donovan Ltd. (Ryde Garage), Victoria Street, Ryde was the Isle of Wight's main dealer for Standard, Triumph and Lancia cars in the 1940s and 1950s in large, purpose-built premises. The business was sold to Shotters Ltd. around 1960. The garage has since been demolished and replaced by a pay and display car park. Mr de Castel-Branco of Ryde bought at least three cars from Downing and Donovan in the 1930s and 1940s and took the two photographs above. They include views of his Triumph Renown saloon GDL 107, which was new in May 1949. (Carisbrooke Castle Museum)

External view of J.B. Eames' garage, Sandown, c.1939. (Thomas, Sandown)

J.B. Eames, Station Avenue, Sandown was a major garage near the town centre. When this promotional postcard was produced, probably just before WW2, J.B. (Jim) Eames was the Isle of Wight dealer for BSA cars. Jim's brother H.G. Eames was a successful coach operator at Shanklin up to 1937 when he sold his business including 13 coaches to Southern Vectis. All of Eames' coaches carried DL registrations and most were manufactured by Dennis in Guildford.

(Thomas, Shanklin)

P.J. Duff (Winchester Park garage), Fitzroy Street, Sandown was possibly Sandown's largest garage in the 1940s and 1950s. Situated in the heart of the town this business served many of the town's hoteliers, offering a wide range of sales, service, repairs and forecourt facilities. These two promotional postcard views were probably taken on the same day just before WW2. The car at the front of both pictures, DL 8545, is a Vauxhall Light Six. It was first registered on 25th July 1933 to an owner in Niton.

Internal view of P.J. Duff's garage (Thomas, Shanklin)

G.K. Nash's petrol filling station, Ventnor

G.K. Nash owned several garage premises in Ventnor and Niton in the 1940s, 1950s and 1960s. This family business was a dealer for Morris and Citroen cars and provided a wide range of motor services to local residents and businesses. The top photograph shows G.K. Nash's showroom and offices in Pier Street (now a Co-op supermarket) and the lower picture shows Nash's petrol filling station in Victoria Street (which would become a small bus station). (Upper photo Ventnor Heritage Centre archives; lower photo copyright W.J. Nigh and Sons Ltd., Shanklin, IW)

The above copyright photograph was taken by Stanley Nigh of W.J. Nigh and Sons, Ltd. in the summer of 1955. It shows brand new Morris Isis MDL 291 plus two new Morris Minor Series II cars in G.K. Nash's showroom in Ventnor. MDL 291 was purchased by Stanley Nigh and it appears in a number of Nigh postcard view which were taken by him during the 1950s.

M. Millmore Ltd., High Street, Ventnor was a long established transport firm. The Millmore family had operated a carrier business between Ventnor and Newport for several generations. Millmore had a fleet of large vans based at his garage at the edge of the town centre. This garage concentrated on vehicle repairs and petrol sales with the sale of some second hand vehicles. (Ventnor Heritage Centre)

Brighstone Service Station, Military Road, Brighstone. This photograph, taken around 1960, shows an example of a rural Isle of Wight petrol filling station. The business concentrated mainly on the sale of petrol, oil and a limited range of motoring accessories. At the rear of the picture 1958 Vauxhall Victor estate car PDL 957 may be seen at one of the pumps. (copyright W.J. Nigh and Sons Ltd., Shanklin, IW)

Chale Green general store and petrol filling station. This postcard photo was taken either just before or after WW2. Austin Seven Ruby saloon ADL 972 was new in 1936. Part of the message on the rear of the card, posted in August 1946, reads "Dear Mum and Dad. This is a picture of where we are staying. The shop is a garage, grocers, greengrocers, butchers, newsagent, tobacconist, confectioners, post office, in fact everything, milk as well. We did about 26 miles yesterday on the bike (tandem) to Alum Bay, where the coloured sands are. Jim and Molly." (Author's collection)

Brighstone village petrol filling station was probably one of the smallest on the Island. This photograph was taken by Stanley Nigh in 1955 or 1956. Mr Nigh's Morris Isis MDL 291 may be seen in the picture and the two bus stops probably belong to Shotters Ltd. who operated a popular local bus service from St Thomas' Square, Newport to Brighstone and Compton Bay up to May 1956. (Copyright W.J. Nigh and Sons Ltd., Shanklin, IW)

Appendix 3 – DDL-registered buses produced during WW2

DDL 50 Bristol K5G with Eastern Coachworks H56R bodywork. New to Southern Vectis. First registered 1/1/1940. Converted to open top bus in 1959. Converted to tree lopper in 1969. Sold in 1979. Privately restored and preserved as open top bus by Derek Priddle. This vintage vehicle is often on display at the Isle of Wight Bus and Coach Museum in Ryde.

DDL 51 Bristol L5G with Eastern Coachworks B35R bodywork. New to Southern Vectis. First registered 1/1/1940. Withdrawn in 1957.

DDL 52 Bristol L5G with Eastern Coachworks B35R bodywork. New to Southern Vectis. First registered 1/1/1940. Withdrawn in 1957.

DDL 53 Bristol L5G with Eastern Coachworks B35R bodywork. New to Southern Vectis. First registered 1/1/1940. Withdrawn in 1957.

DDL 54 Bristol L5G with Eastern Coachworks B35R bodywork. New to Southern Vectis. First registered 1/1/1940. Withdrawn in 1957.

DDL 531 Bedford OWB with Duple UB32F bodywork. Supplied by Canning Day Ltd., Newport. New to R.S. Lane, Lane's and Davies Ltd., Shanklin (G.A. Shotter). First registered 12/3/1943. Subsequently owned by Shotters Ltd., Shanklin from 11/46 to 1954.

DDL 532 Bedford OWB with Duple UB32F bodywork. Supplied by Canning Day Ltd., Newport. New to Enterprise (J.H. Wavell), Newport. First registered 1/2/1943. Subsequently owned by Southern Vectis from 1951 to 1954

DDL 586 Bedford OWB with Duple UB32F bodywork. New to G.A. Shotter (W.C. and R.P. Shotter), Brighstone. First registered 4/6/1943. Sold in 1949.

DDL 649 Bedford OWB with Duple UB32F bodywork. Supplied by Canning Day Ltd., Newport. New to Seaview Services, Ltd. First registered 3/4/1944. Sold in 3/1954

DDL 662 Bedford OWB with Duple UB32F bodywork. Supplied by Canning Day Ltd., Newport. New to Seaview Services, Ltd. First registered 3/4/1944. Sold in 3/1954

DDL 688 Bristol K6A/ later K5G with Park Royal UH56R bodywork. New to Southern Vectis. First registered 29/12/1944. Rebodied by Eastern Coachworks L55R in 1953. Withdrawn in 1967.

DDL 706 Bedford OWB with Duple UB32F bodywork. Supplied by Canning Day Ltd., Newport. New to Randall, Ventnor. First registered 1/9/1944. Sold to Enterprise (J.H. Wavell), Newport 6/1949 then resold to SV in 6/1951. Withdrawn in 1954.

DDL 759 Bristol K6A/ later K5G with Park Royal UH56R bodywork. New to Southern Vectis. First registered 30/6/1945. Rebodied by Eastern Coachworks L55R in 1953. Withdrawn in 1967.

DDL 764 Bristol K6A/ later K5G with Duple UH56R bodywork. New to Southern Vectis. First registered 30/6/1945. Rebodied by Eastern Coachworks L55R in 1953. Withdrawn in 1967.

DDL 765 Bristol K6A/ later K5G with Duple UH56R bodywork. New to Southern Vectis. First registered 14/9/1945. Rebodied by Eastern Coachworks L55R in 1953. Withdrawn in 1968.

Appendix 4 – Motor vehicles built on the Island

Prior to 1939 there had been several vehicle manufacturers and coachbuilders on the Isle of Wight. These included the Liquid Fuel Engineering Company in East Cowes (1896 to 1900), Gilbert Campling Ltd.'s ABC Skootamota at Somerton (1918 to 1922) and a number of small and medium sized coachbuilders (e.g. R. Bird Cheverton and Co. Ltd. and Harry Margham and Sons Ltd. in Newport, and George H. Mullis and Co. and Pollard and Sons in Ryde). It has not been possible to identify any complete motor vehicles which were manufactured or assembled on the Island during the period 1939 to 1964. It should of course be noted that this was a very busy time for the design and construction of many ships, yachts and aircraft plus the early development of the hovercraft, especially in Cowes and East Cowes.

The two main coachbuilding firms on the Isle of Wight in the 1940s and 1950s were undoubtedly Harry Margham and Sons Ltd. and Frank Cheverton Ltd., both of whom were located in Newport. Marghams specialised in the design, construction and repair of bodies for coaches and commercial vehicles. The last two coaches bodied by the firm were FDL 67 (a 35-seat Daimler CVD6 for Shotters Ltd. of Brighstone) in 1948 and GDL 58 (a 29-seat Commer Commando for Holmes Saloon Coaches of Cowes) in 1949. Marghams built bodies for a variety of vehicles. Large numbers of caravans were produced in the Crocker Street workshops in the 1950s and van and lorry bodies continued to be manufactured up to 1968. The final commercial vehicles to be bodied by the firm were three flatbed lorries for Whitbread's.

Frank Cheverton Ltd. was the only other significant coachbuilder on the Island in the 1940s and 1950s. During the Second World War the firm became government engineering contractors. The original motor shop was converted to a machine shop and fitted out with capstan lathes, millers, etc. and the latest machine shop equipment. The firm obtained Air Ministry approval and was entrusted with Part 1 work for this Ministry. Contracts were also received from the Ministry of Supply and the Admiralty. 45 people were employed in this department, including 35 women, and further workshops had to be built to accommodate the work. Millions of stainless steel bolts and aircraft fittings were manufactured, and many thousands of complete sets of pontoon fittings were supplied to pontoon manufacturers throughout the country. In addition the tractor and agriculture departments expanded rapidly to meet ever increasing wartime demands for new tractors and related equipment and to keep existing machines at work.

After the war Chevertons resumed their coachbuilding, painting and lettering work. This particularly involved building and fitting bodies for vans and trucks from 5cwt to 6 tons capacity. Many special bodies were provided, including a Chevertons' Ford shooting brake model. The firm also undertook a large amount of body repair work on cars and commercial vehicles. This became an increasingly important part of the firm's business in the 1960s.

Apart from Marghams and Chevertons there are very few known examples of other coachbuilders in this period. One exception was Southern Vectis which carried out the conversion of two of its double deck Bristol K5G buses in 1959 into open top vehicles for use on coastal sightseeing routes for summer visitors (CDL 899 and DDL 50). Southern Vectis rebodied many of its 1940s single deck and double deck buses in the 1950s but this work was normally carried out on the mainland. The only other known 'coachbuilder' was the former Newport brewery W.B. Mew Langton and Co. Ltd. In 1949 the firm took delivery of a large flatbed Seddon lorry which was supplied with the registration number GCR 447 by Seddon's nearest agent in Southampton. Using their own vehicle maintenance staff Mew Langtons carried out certain sturdy adaptations to the rear section of this vehicle, to make it more suitable for carrying beer barrels, crates of bottles, and other bulky items. Although it is not DL-registered this vehicle has spent virtually all its life on the Island. Please refer to the post-war austerity chapter for further details of this unusual commercial vehicle which still exists and is in good running order.

Appendix 5 – Suppliers of prestige DL registrations

ADL 1	Stratstones Ltd., October 1935 (1st owner Sir S. Hanson Rowbotham, Brighstone)
BDL 1	Frank Cheverton Ltd., Newport, January 1937
CDL 1	Frank Cheverton Ltd., Newport, April 1938
DDL 1	P.J. Duff, Sandown, September 1939
EDL 1	Frank Cheverton Ltd., Newport, March 1946 (Austin 8 saloon owned by a Mr Day)
FDL 1	Frank Cheverton Ltd., Newport, July 1947
GDL 1	L.V. Floyd, March 1949
HDL 1	Bellevue Garage Ltd., Ryde, August 1950 (1949 Vauxhall Velox ?)
JDL 1	Frank Cheverton Ltd., Newport, March 1952
KDL 1	Southern Vectis Omnibus Company Ltd., July 1953 (Bristol Lodekka double deck bus)
LDL 1	Fowlers (IW) Ltd., Newport, July 1954
MDL 1	Frank Cheverton Ltd., Newport, May 1955
NDL 1	H.J. Aedy, East Cowes, March 1956
ODL 1	Frank Cheverton Ltd., Newport, January 1957
PDL 1	Wadham Brothers Ltd., Northwood, September 1957
RDL 1	Frank Cheverton Ltd., Newport, May 1958
SDL 1	H.J. Aedy, East Cowes, January 1959
TDL 1	Frank Cheverton Ltd., Newport, July 1959
UDL 1	Frank Cheverton Ltd., Newport, February 1960
VDL 1	Totland Service Station Ltd., July 1960 (Mary Lady Tennyson Daimler ambulance, Freshwater)
WDL 1	Frank Cheverton Ltd., Newport, March 1961
XDL 1	Frank Cheverton Ltd., Newport, August 1961
YDL 1	Canning Day Ltd., Newport, April 1962 (Austin Westminster ?)
1 ADL	Frank Cheverton Ltd., Newport, November 1962
1 BDL	Frank Cheverton Ltd., Newport, May 1963
1 CDL	Frank Cheverton, Ltd., Newport, October 1963

(Copyright Brian Botley)

n.b. Most of these registrations are currently in use as cherished number plates.

Appendix 6 – Some examples of cherished DL registration numbers

For many years some people have chosen to retain or transfer old Isle of Wight registration numbers and to use them on their current cars. This is done for a variety of reasons. Some people like to have personalised plates to coincide with their initials or the name of their company. Others wish to demonstrate the Isle of Wight's historic connection with the DL code. Another reason in the past was that the car ferry operators used to offer discounted tickets for travellers across the Solent who had DL-registered vehicles. In recent years, following the introduction of the controversial HW Isle of Wight code in 2001, cherished pre-1964 DL numbers appear to have become even more popular. For lots of people DL plates reinforce and perpetuate this highly valued element of the Isle of Wight's identity.

The main focus of this book is on motor vehicles with original DL registrations but it seems appropriate to mention this significant aspect of the overall subject. Perhaps one day another author may choose to write a book devoted entirely to cherished DL registration numbers.

Felix Hetherington, the Chairman of the County Press Board of Trustees and a former Chief Executive of Isle of Wight Council, has owned the registration VDL 175 since 1983. At that time the registration number was attached to a 1960 Austin A40 Farina which was in very poor condition. Felix arranged the transfer of VDL 175 to his car, a VW Golf GTi. During the past 30 years Felix has transferred this cherished registration number to several other cars he has owned, including a Mercedes 190, a BMW 320, a BMW convertible 328, a Porsche convertible and a Jaguar XJ. The following photographs taken by the owner show the VDL 175 plate on three of these cars.

Somewhat unsurprisingly, the first known cherished DL registration number was DL 1. According to an article in the County Press in the 1980s this was purchased by a Mr Whaley in the 1920s. Driving past H.B. Jolliffe's scrapyard in Somerton, near Cowes, Mr Whaley noticed the distinctive plate attached to a wrecked de Dion Bouton car. He paid £5 for the number. It was then transferred and used by his family on many different cars for over 60 years. Some other very early DL registrations which are known to be in use as cherished number plates are DL 3, DL 5, DL 6, DL 7, DL9, DL 11, DL 14, DL 18, DL 20, DL 21, DL 40, DL 44, DL 45, DL 47, DL 48 and DL 50.

Another example of a cherished DL registration number is KDL 1. This number was originally issued in July 1953 to Southern Vectis for a Bristol Lodekka double deck bus. The bus was sold in the 1970s. Around that time the number KDL 1 is believed to have been transferred to a 1950s Humber Hawk car (see photo below). This photograph was taken by Graham Hindle at the Enfield Pageant of Motoring in 1999.

References

Allen, P.C. and MacLeod, A.B., *Rails in the Isle of Wight,* David and Charles, 1986

Chessell, Mark P., *Independent Bus Services on the Isle of Wight*, Chine Publishing, 2012

Chessell, Mark P., *DL: Isle of Wight Motor Vehicles 1896 – 1939,* Chine Publishing, 2014

Frank Cheverton Ltd., Newport, Isle of Wight, *A Century of Progress 1852 – 1952,* 1952

Daily Mail Motorcycling Guide, Associated Newspapers Ltd., 1953

Facebook page 'DL Isle of Wight registrations'

Fallick, Norman, *Unpublished life story 1928 to 2017,* 2017

Isle of Wight County Press, various issues of this weekly local newspaper from 1939 to 2017

Isle of Wight Record Office, *original Isle of Wight County Council DL-registration ledgers,* covering the period November 1926 to February 1964

Jones, Terry, *Shotters Ltd. of Brighstone, Isle of Wight: An illustrated fleet and company history,* published by author, 2014

Newman, Richard, *Southern Vectis: the first 60 years,* published by Ensign Publications, Southampton for Southern Vectis, 1989

Relf, Peter, *Yahoo Groups DL Photos website*

Searle, Adrian, *Isle of Wight at War 1939 – 1945,* The Dovecote Press, 1989

Vincent, Don and Jones, Terry, *Isle of Wight Registrations bus and coach ('PSV') issues, three-letter '_DL' series, 1936 to 1974,* published by Don Vincent, 2016

Vincent, Don and Roberts, Chris, *Isle of Wight registrations in the original DL-series, DL 1 to DL 9999 (1903 to 1935), 2nd edition 2008 with 2010 supplement*

Wikipedia online reports on various makes and models of motor vehicles

Woodall, Noel and Heaton, Brian, *Car Numbers then and now,* Registrations Publications, 2008